In the Latter Days

An Intellectually Honest Study of Bible Prophecies
Concerning End Times

by

Thomas O. Meeker

Email: ThomasOMeeker@gmail.com

Table of Contents

Table of Figures

Please Note:

To get the most out of this study you must have a Bible at hand and you must read it. If you are not familiar with the makeup of the Bible or the narrative of human history it provides, you may struggle to understand the words of prophecy in context. At the very least, before you begin a chapter in this book, you must read the Bible texts listed at the beginning of each chapter. Otherwise, you will not be able to fully grasp the bigger picture of what you are discovering. Also, in order to save space, I seldom wrote out the Bible texts being discussed. So you will need to keep your Bible right next to you and refer to the texts often as you progress through the studies.

I use the King James Version of the Bible almost exclusively in this study and any quotes in this book come from that Bible. Other versions of the Bible can be employed by the reader and used successfully if it is kept in mind that modern translations that attempt to make the Bible more "understandable" generally do so by presenting the "understanding" that the authors and translators have. In other words, they take the words of the Bible and attempt to explain what *the authors* believe the text means in as simple a way as possible. As will be explained in more detail in the introduction, these simplifications are based on the translator's *assumptions* concerning the meaning of the text and all too often begin to reflect the translator's personal doctrinal biases. Because of this, I have little use for the many recently published English translations of the Bible. The King James Bible is not without some of the same issues. Nevertheless, I believe it is still the most accurate English translation available and most of its quirks are known and correctable by referencing the original language dictionaries (Hebrew and Greek) in Strong's Concordance.

I pray that you will enjoy this book and will be enlightened by it.

Introduction:

 As I set out to write a book about End Times Prophecy one of the most important rules of interpretation that must be carefully observed is to distinguish between what is actually said in the texts and that which is assumption, exaggeration, speculation or imagination.

All too often writers and preachers of prophecy publish their works mainly because they believe they have solved the riddle or completed the picture. But their resulting product ends up being more a description of their own personal opinions, assumptions, speculations and biases than of what the writings actually say. That by itself wouldn't be so bad. The problem comes when these assumptions and speculations are not presented as such, but rather are presented and accepted as though they are well established truth. Presenting them this way implies that the conclusions of the author have been proven from the Bible and are sure, when in fact they are not.

I believe this is the same mistake the Pharisees made in Jesus' day. They had studied the prophets of old concerning the coming of Christ, even memorized them. But with that they made assumptions about what his coming would be like, turned those assumptions into doctrine and facts, and taught these "facts" for centuries. The assumptions had become the truth in their minds. Thus, when Jesus came and did not fulfill these "truths," they were compelled to reject him and thus missed the "time of their visitation." (Luke 19:44)

In hopes of avoiding this kind of error I have carefully tried to distinguish in this study between the facts from the writings of the Bible and the assumptions or speculations that may be made from them. The facts from prophecy are unmovable and sure. Any assumptions or speculations must be open for change or outright abandonment if events around us prove them wrong.

Now, I understand that "facts" can also be open to interpretation and interpretation can be a very subjective thing. Therefore, an author's *method* of interpretation is extremely important if he hopes to discover what is true. The method should be as objective as possible and designed to remove the natural tendency to project one's own biases or preconceptions into the interpretation. The goal is to allow prophecy to define what is true and to paint its own prophetic picture of what is to come. The goal is not to *use* the Bible to support or lend credence to one's own pet doctrines or preconceived beliefs or imaginations. Sadly, the latter approach is more often than not the method that is applied in prophetic studies.

In this study I begin with the assumption that I know nothing of the subject at hand. I approach the prophecies of the Bible like a detective looking for clues to solve a mystery. In order to get to the truth, I have to trust that my clues are accurate and that they say what they mean and mean what they say. But like every human being it is hard not to filter what I'm seeing subjectively. So in an attempt to keep my method of interpretation as objective as possible, I developed several ground rules.

First, I only know something for sure if it is stated in prophecy. If it is not clearly stated in prophecy, then it is not known for sure. If a verse is vague or unclear, then it must be left that way; vague and unclear. The interpretation of such a verse must be left open and undefined unless there is something else found in the writings that specifically explains its meaning. Anything we discover that is unclear or beyond the writings of the Bible must be held as speculation and subject to error.

Second, I do not exaggerate, stretch, spiritualize or project the meaning of prophecies. Unless there are other specifically related verses that make it *plain* that there is a larger or deeper meaning to a text, I take the text for what it says and leave it at that. For example, if a verse says, "The day of the Lord" I interpret it to mean a literal "day" and not a general period of time or a dispensation of time. Unless the surrounding context makes it *plain* that it means a general period of time, I will interpret the text to mean what it says…a day.

Next, I do not isolate scriptures. This is a technique often and commonly applied where the author takes a few seemingly related verses and uses them to make a point or support an idea while conveniently ignoring other verses that conflict, contradict or even refute the claim. In other words, they isolate the supporting scriptures from the rest of the writings. Since the Bible is a huge book and few people actually have a good handle on what is and what is not contained in the book it is easy for authors to do this. Sometimes this happens because of the author's own ignorance of the Bible, but sometimes it appears to be intentional in order to promote the authors own prejudicial biases or doctrinal claims. That's when the approach becomes intellectually dishonest. I believe that all of the prophecy in the Bible is true and accurate. Therefore, it will never contradict itself. If it appears to contradict itself, then there is something we are missing or misunderstanding. If this assumption that prophecy will not contradict itself is a valid assumption, and I believe it is, then there is never a reason to isolate a prophetic text from the rest of the writings. They should all agree and form a congruent picture.

I have been very careful not to isolate any scriptures in this writing. As I progressed through the study I searched diligently for texts that might conflict with or contradict the picture as I understood it. I am still doing this today. Since I know the prophecies of the Bible are true and therefore congruent in all their statements, whenever I find something that appears to conflict I have to figure out what I am missing. In most cases when I go deeper into the original languages I am usually able to discover the error. But in no case do I attempt to force the writings to confirm my own subjective biases. Rather, I allow the prophecies to paint the picture for me and am determined to alter what I believe is true to accommodate all that is written about the subject. As I did this a wonderful congruent picture of the timeline of events began to come together easily and understandably with no contradicting or conflicting texts to be explained away. Not everything is understood perfectly. In fact, there is a lot that is not understood clearly, especially when you get to the more symbolic texts. But at this point as I continue my search in the writings, I am no longer finding texts that conflict with the picture or timeline that has come forth.

My next ground rule is that I take the words of prophecy literally unless it is *plain* in the context that the things being said are symbolic. For example, when Daniel says he sees a beast with seven heads and ten horns coming out of the sea, it is clear that this is symbolic. But when the angel says the ten horns represent ten kings, it is clear he means ten literal kings or rulers. Symbolism is one of the danger zones for interpretation. When something is symbolic it is all too easy for the author to make it say whatever he wants. In some cases the prophecy itself tells you what the symbols stand for but in many cases it does not. I will never claim to know what a symbolic picture or element in the picture stands for unless the prophecy tells me specifically. There is a lot of room to speculate, and that is fine. I do offer speculations at times. But the reader should be very wary of any author that flatly claims to know what a symbol stands for. It is very easy to project one's own doctrinal biases or preconceived ideas into these pictures and with no texts to define them the reader is hard put to refute the claims. All too often the reader is left to assume that the author got his information from some other "reliable" source. The reader should be very wary of such claims no matter how educated or credentialed the author may be.

Lastly, I approach the writings with the belief that the texts of the Bible were written for the common man, and, though there are, no doubt, deeper meanings and mysteries that are not immediately obvious, I believe one does not have to be an intellectual versed in all of the history, languages, culture and literature of the time to understand the clear messages of the gospel and of prophecy. One has only to be a careful student of the writings and a temple of the Holy Ghost. In fact, my experience has taught me that those who try too hard to find deep hidden interpretations or meanings in the Bible generally end up "discovering" amazingly complex "truths" that have broad implications and apparent applications... but are built entirely on assumption. In spite of this intellectual dishonesty, it seems these "truths" somehow manage to become widely accepted as doctrinal positions. These positions, then, have resulted in sects, cults, denominations and various other divisions in the churches. The sad part is that many if not most of these doctrinal stances or positions are ultimately based on nothing more than assumption, exaggeration, speculation and the imagination of the inventers' own hearts, which are then received with itching ears (2 Tim. 4:3-4).

Therefore, this book is not presented as or intended to be a "scholarly" work. I am generally familiar with most of the many and varied inventions that theologians have created to explain the hidden meanings of the symbolic pictures described in these prophecies. But I am of the mind to believe that such "knowledge" is not necessary to get a clear picture of what is to come. So, in this work you will find me occasionally saying, "I don't know what that means," or "I don't think it matters if we don't know what this means." Don't let that bother you. As we work through the prophecies you will find that there are a tremendous number of definite clearly stated facts that we can learn that give us a well defined chronology of the latter days, even without knowing what each detail of the symbolic pictures stands for.

Basically what I am going to be focusing on is developing a timeline. Using just what the writings and the prophecies in the writings tell us, without exaggerating, reaching, stretching, spiritualizing, symbolizing, isolating, projecting or looking for hidden meanings, we will discover amazing detail and congruence as to the chronology of events. Once we understand the chronology and the framework, even if we do not fully understand what the events are or exactly how they will look, we will be equipped to recognize the events when they actually begin to happen, and thus will not miss our time of visitation. (Luke 21:28)

As a final note, I *am* going to make some speculations and guesses in this study. The key is to be very careful to distinguish between what is speculation and what is not. As the study progresses, you will find references to, "The Maybe Box." This is where all of the speculations are kept. It's alright to have a Maybe Box. Just remember that things in this box could be wrong and must be held lightly. As history unfolds, things in the Maybe Box may be confirmed, modified or contradicted. We must be willing to allow those things to be denied or changed as events of future history dictate.

Our journey begins in the book of Daniel where most of the framework of the timeline is discovered. Then we will move on to the words of Jesus in the gospels of Matthew, Mark and Luke. With this knowledge, then, we will work our way through the Book of Revelation and will discover that we are much better equipped to understand how these things flow into the chronology of events In the Latter Days.

1. The Statue of Nebuchadnezzar's Dream: Daniel Chapter 2

To begin this chapter, read chapters 1 and 2 in the Book of Daniel.

In Daniel Chapter 2, we have the dream of Nebuchadnezzar, king of Babylon, of the great statue made of many metals. Since Nebuchadnezzar could not remember the dream, he called for all of his wise men to reveal the dream but they could not. Nebuchadnezzar decreed that all of the wise men should be destroyed because of this, but Daniel came on the scene and through a revelation of God, not only revealed the dream but also gave its interpretation.

This vision is the first hint for us as to the plan of God for man on the earth. It gives us a broad overview of the five kingdoms of man that will "rule over all the earth" (2:39) followed by the Kingdom of God which shall reign for ever and ever.

The heart of the matter begins at Daniel 2:28 and continues to 2:45. In a nut shell, the dream was of a statue whose head was made of gold, his chest and arms of silver, his torso and thighs of brass, his legs of iron and his feet and toes made of iron mixed with clay. In the dream a stone was "cut out without hands" (2:34) that smote the image on its feet breaking the entire statue to pieces which turned to chaff and blew away in the wind. Then the stone grew into a great mountain that filled the whole earth.

After describing the dream, Daniel goes on to give the interpretation of it (2:36). He describes the various parts of the statue as representing kingdoms on the earth with the first one, the head of gold, representing Nebuchadnezzar and Babylon. After him will come another kingdom inferior to him, and then a third kingdom of brass. And then there is a fourth kingdom of iron which breaks in pieces all things and obviously will be a very oppressive kingdom.

As for the feet and toes of iron and clay, it is interesting to note that Daniel does not call it the "fifth" kingdom but simply refers to it as "the kingdom." (2:41) I don't know if that is significant or not and would be reluctant to make anything of it. But moving for a moment to the Maybe Box, some suggest that this implies a continuance of the 4th kingdom. The

11

fact that the feet and toes are part of iron like the fourth kingdom also suggests this to them. However, the description of the kingdom represented by the feet and toes is very different from the description of the fourth kingdom which would suggest that it is a completely separate kingdom. Though I believe it to be a separate kingdom, the thing I would encourage you to keep in mind is that this is one statue and that all of the kingdoms represent a single image and are thus part of each other. In other words, they emanate from a single "spirit." I will have more to say on this later.

At the time Daniel was giving the interpretation of the dream to the king, all of the events and kingdoms described except for the head of gold were future. Today, however, some twenty six hundred years later, much of the vision is history. Thus, we can easily identify and verify many of the truths that are revealed in the dream.

The head of gold represented Babylon and king Nebuchadnezzar (2:38) which ran from about 605 BC to around 562 BC. After that came the empire of the Meads and the Persians, the silver, and ran from about 538 BC to 330 BC. The Greeks and Alexander the Great, the brass, followed next from 330 BC to about 323 BC. The Greek empire under one king was short lived because Alexander the Great died at the young age of 32. Following the Greeks was a period of about 100 years when there was no great world dominating empire. But by around 250 BC the Romans were beginning to come to power. Over the next 200 years, the Romans continued to conquer nation after nation, people after people until by about 50 BC they controlled virtually the entire known world. This would be the legs of iron. The Roman Empire continued for some 500 years after that, not breaking apart until around 420 AD.

Since the Roman Empire broke apart there has never again been a kingdom of men that ruled the entire world. For the next fifteen hundred and ninety years to the present (2011), the world has been split apart into dozens of peoples, nations, countries and groups. Therefore, the last kingdom of men represented in Nebuchadnezzar's statue, that will rule the world, *must be future.*

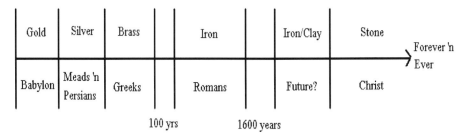

Figure 1: The Kingdoms of Men in Daniel 2

The very fact that the last two kingdoms of men are separated by at least 1600 years flies in the face of the idea that the fifth kingdom represented in the statue is just a continuation of the fourth. However, this does not preclude the idea that governmental, cultural and spiritual characteristics of the Roman Empire could be carried down through the centuries to this last kingdom. Clearly influences of thought, culture and principles of government and finance were passed down from Babylon to the Meads and Persians and from there to the Greeks and from the Greeks to the many peoples of the Roman Empire. Cultural norms are passed from generation to generation and are never really lost even though different kings and kingdoms come and go in power. Some things do change over time but the spiritual underpinnings of man do not change…unless they come to the redeeming knowledge of Christ.

So this is the picture of the five kingdoms of men that will rule over all the earth. These are the *anti-kingdoms*. I call them anti-kingdoms because the true King of all is Christ and of His Kingdom there shall be no end. Thus we begin to see that the anti-kingdoms of men are antichrist and are an attempt by men to rule over all the earth in place of the true King, Jesus.

From this picture I believe we can begin to say that one of the basic underlying characteristics of the spirit of antichrist is that it desires to rule the world. This is an important characteristic to understand and to remember because even today there are factions within the Christian Church that would persuade you to believe that the ultimate destiny of the Church is to rule the world for Christ…*before* his return. Indeed there are some factions that believe when the Church takes over and rules the world; this *constitutes* the return of Christ. They justify this by saying the Church is the body of Christ and thus, as his body, when we rule he rules. Be careful of these lies and recognize that any spirit that says it is it's destiny to rule the world is of the spirit of antichrist.

Jesus said to Pilate in John 18:36, "My kingdom is not of this world. If my kingdom were of this world, then would my servants fight, that I should not be delivered to the Jews: but now is my kingdom not from hence." If Jesus said his kingdom is not of this world, and that his servants should not fight because of this, why do any in the Church today believe that this has changed and we should now strive to rule over the kingdoms of men? In my view, we shouldn't. Such things are not of Christ, they are anti-Christ.

So now let's talk more about this future kingdom of men represented by the feet and toes of iron and clay. Since this kingdom is future the only things we know about it come from the prophecy. Anything beyond the prophecy must go into the Maybe Box until or unless other texts in the writings confirm such ideas. For now, here are the things we know about this kingdom from Daniel chapter 2.

All of the kingdoms preceding the feet and toes were of a pure metal. This kingdom is mixed with iron and clay which Daniel says means the kingdom shall be divided (2:41). This makes it "different" from the others. The government of this kingdom, though strong, is not fully unified. The fact that it is "different" is important to note because this comes up in subsequent prophecies. The preceding kingdoms all had a single king or a single ruling authority with the conquered lands being unified under that single ruler into a single political or governmental system. It should also be noted that these first four kingdoms were all created militarily by wars and military conquest. The nations that were conquered were *forced* to become part of the conquering kingdom. This last kingdom, however, will apparently have several kings at once while the peoples under them, though "mingling," will not be unified. It is implied that not even the kings of this last kingdom will be unified with one another. We know that there is to be more than one king because of verse 44 which makes reference to them in the plural. We also know there is to be more than one king because of subsequent prophecies yet to be examined in Daniel and Revelation. As we move forward through subsequent chapters of this book and others in the Bible, we will discover, in fact, that there are to be ten kings that rule simultaneously during this last kingdom. This fits very nicely with the ten toes of Daniel chapter 2. Daniel 2 does not specifically identify the toes as kings, so at this point in our journey that would be an assumption. However, in verses 41 and 42 of the chapter the toes are specifically pointed out which suggests their symbolism is significant. In our next chapter, Daniel chapter 7, we find this assumption confirmed with no stretching or exaggerating of prophecy.

Moving for a moment to the Maybe Box, as we think about how this last kingdom might be consolidated, it seems increasingly unlikely that it will form as a result of military conquest. If we look at the world's condition militarily today, it seems unlikely that any super power could conquer the whole world militarily because of the potential for nuclear retaliation, which would assure the mutual destruction of all. Therefore, it seems much more likely that any world governance of the near future would come to power through political intrigue, manipulation and treaties. In reality, this is one of the trends we see developing in the governments of the world today under the guise of controlling global warming or the global economy. Everyone is talking about the "need" for global governance.

But, to summarize, here are the things we know *for sure* about this fifth and last kingdom of men:

1. There is a future kingdom of men that will essentially rule over all the earth.
2. This kingdom will be divided (vs. 41). It will not be a united kingdom as all the others were.
3. This kingdom will have the strength of iron (41) which suggests it will be brutal and oppressive as was the Roman Empire.
4. It will be partly strong and partly broken or "fragile" as it says in some Bible versions. (42) It will be divided and not unified even though it rules with iron.
5. The people of this kingdom will "mingle" or intermarry but the various people groups will not "cleave" to one another or be unified. (43)
6. Verse 44 refers to "these kings." Though it does not state it here overtly, it is made clear in other verses (Daniel 7:24 and Rev. 17:12) that there are ten kings in the last kingdom. This would seem to fit nicely with the ten toes of the statue that are pointed out in verses 41 and 42.
7. This will be the last kingdom of men which will be destroyed by the "stone."

Following this fifth and last kingdom of men there is to be a sixth kingdom set up by the God of Heaven (2:44) that will stand forever and break in pieces all of the kingdoms of men. Here are the things we know for sure from prophecy about this sixth kingdom:

1. It is set up by God (44).
2. It will never be destroyed (44).
3. It will not be left to other people (44); which I think means there will never again be another king. In other words, this king will not die and leave the kingdom to another people.
4. It will break in pieces and consume all the kingdoms of men (44).
5. It will stand forever. (44)
6. It is made without hands (45); which means it is not man made but made by God.
7. It is of "stone" cut out without hands and unformed which is distinguished from metals and clay that are formed with men's hands.

Now that we have some facts about this last kingdom let's do some more speculating in our Maybe Box. Are there any events or conditions of our modern day world that would lead us to believe we could be nearing the fulfillment of this prophecy? Let's take a look.

It is interesting to note in the news how the nations of the world, including the US with the election of Barak Obama as president, are now attempting to form a global "governance" which will be given sovereignty over one or more aspects of global concern. There have been conferences held to accomplish this, the first of which was held in Copenhagen and the most recent of which was in Cancun. An attempt was made at the Copenhagen conference to form a world controlling sovereign committee under the guise of dealing with global climate change. The reality is, the formation of this global "committee" was and is itself the real goal and they are unconcerned for what world crisis, real or manufactured, it is formed around. I believe they will use any global issue, whether it be climate, the economy, a pandemic or the threat of global war, to justify the formation of this governing body.

I saw a rough draft of the treaty that was being presented in Copenhagen. Basically it would form a committee populated by an unspecified number of directors from various countries who would be given authority to make decisions on the issue at hand. The various nations of the world would have to sign on to this treaty which would then subjugate their sovereignty in these areas of concern to the committee. Once this committee is formed and nations sign away their sovereignty in any area of concern, the die will be cast for global government and power will begin to flow to it.

This committee could easily be made of ten principle directors. They would unite with incredible power to control various aspects of the world because of the treaty. However, being of different nations and backgrounds, the individual directors or kings would, no doubt, still have their own self interests and those of their nation at heart and thus would not truly be united. Though the Copenhagen conference ended with no signed treaty, much was learned from it. And this type of endeavor could easily be successful and come about within the next year or two. This would be a fitting fulfillment of Daniel chapter 2.

Another idea, which makes a lot of sense to me, is the growing understanding that there are actually three major entities that are vying for world domination. This would be the Muslims who are attempting to form a world Caliphate, the Communists who are attempting to use unions and Marxist principles to gain control of the people, and the elites of the world in governments and the UN who intend to control the world through pure power and money or "the new world order." These three groups are now apparently working together to bring down capitalism through the collapse of the United States and the destruction of Israel. This would definitely fit the description of iron and clay as presented by Daniel because though these entities may be working together, they are by no means friends. Though they may end up forming a world government, they will by no means be unified or clinging to one another. The ideologies will never mix.

There are other theories and speculations as to how this prophecy could be fulfilled. The one that is most commonly presented comes from the teachings of Dispensationalism which claims (not presented as speculation) there will be a ten nation confederacy, probably from the European Union, that will join together and rise to power and conquer or control the world. Twenty or more years ago, this idea might have seemed plausible given the conditions of the world but it did not seem to take into account the power of the United States and how it might play into this scenario. Today, with the European Union falling into economic ruin and chaos due to its socialistic governments, it does not appear that this union is going to present any kind of threat to the world as a conquering power. The United States is also falling into economic ruin due to the policies of our new socialistic president, Barak Obama, and soon we, too, may not represent a major player on the world stage. Besides all of this, as mentioned before, because of the proliferation of nuclear weapons throughout the world, the prospect of a successful military take over of the world by any nation or group of nations, without resulting in the total destruction of the world, seems remote. So I would say this theory no longer appears to be viable.

(Author's update, November, 2016. A new president of the United States, Donald Trump, was just elected and will take office this January, 2017. The globalists have still not been able to bring about their one world government, but they are still trying. Mr. Trump is not as sympathetic with the idea of globalism, so possibly there may yet be several years before this global treaty is successfully foisted upon world.)

There are, no doubt, other theories out there but the purpose of this book is not to examine all of the assumptions and ideas put forth as undisputed truth by the various authors, seminaries and teachers of prophecy around the world. Rather, my goal is to emphasize the facts that are stated in prophecy and to distinguish those facts from speculations and assumptions.

2. The Beasts in the Vision: Daniel Chapter 7

Before studying this chapter, you should read chapters 3 through 7 of Daniel.

In Daniel chapter 7 the Lord gives to Daniel a dream or vision that adds more detail to the general timeline revealed in chapter 2. This time the dream or vision comes directly to Daniel. As we go through it you will see that it closely parallels the things we learned in chapter 2 but begins to add more detail to the story.

The nutshell version of the vision is this: Daniel sees the four winds of heaven striving over the great sea. From this sea arise four beasts. He gives a basic description of the first three beasts, and then goes into some greater detail in describing the fourth beast. On the fourth beast some things are happening with the horns. Then comes along the "Ancient of Days" and "one like the son of man" who destroys the fourth beast and gives his body to the "burning fire." The one like the son of man, then, along with the Ancient of Days, sets up a kingdom that lasts for ever and ever.

After the basic vision, the dream continues and Daniel approaches an angel or "one who stood by" to ask him what all of this means. Then the angel proceeds to explain to Daniel all of what he has observed. Again, in a nutshell, the angel explains that the four beasts are four kingdoms. The fourth beast, which is "different" and more dreadful than the others, has ten horns. Then a little horn comes up and uproots three of the ten horns and begins to do terrible things to the "saints," which in Hebrew means, "holy ones." He goes on to describe more about the events surrounding the little horn until the "judgment sits," the beast is destroyed and the Kingdom of God is set up.

So now let's go through this in detail and see what we can learn as good detectives looking for clues. Our main goal is to see if we can form a timeline or see how this new information fits into the existing timeline already discovered in Daniel 2.

The first thing that stands out to me is the statement from the angel that these beasts are four kingdoms. (7:17, 23) We already know from Daniel

2 that there are only five kingdoms of men from the time of Nebuchadnezzar to the end of man's reign on the earth. So, it would be safe to assume without any reaching or stretching of the text of the prophecy that these four kingdoms of Daniel 7 must represent 4 of the 5 kingdoms of Daniel 2; but which ones? Well, let's look at some clues and see if we can make any reasonable matches.

In verse 4 the first beast is described as being like a lion and had eagle's wings. He beheld until the wings were plucked off and the beast was lifted up and made to stand on his feet like a man, and a man's heart was given to him.

I really don't know the significance of the likeness to a lion or the presence of the wings. The color of a lion might be thought of as kind of golden, but I would call that a stretch. But the fact that the wings of the beast were plucked, which means at least that he was grounded, unable to fly or to move swiftly, and afterwards raised up to stand on his feet like a man and given a man's heart, reminds me of the story of Nebuchadnezzar as recorded in Daniel chapter 4.

In Daniel 4 we read the story of how God humbled Nebuchadnezzar by taking away his intelligence and his mind so that he went mad. He was driven from men to live in the field and eat grass like an ox. He was there for seven "times" until his nails grew long and he was covered with hair. After that time, his senses returned to him and he was able to return to his throne and former glory. But the Lord had changed his heart and humbled him so that in 4:37 he confessed, "Now I Nebuchadnezzar praise and extol and honour the King of heaven, all whose works are truth, and his ways judgment: and those that walk in pride he is able to abase."

Nebuchadnezzar had a changed heart and turned from being a proud beast to being a humble man before the Lord. This would seem to fit very nicely with the description of the beast in 7:4 and would tend to suggest that this first beast was indeed Nebuchadnezzar and Babylon. At this point it's just a guess, but would seem to be very reasonable.

The second beast in verse 5 was like a bear which raised itself up on one side and had three ribs in its mouth. It was said to it, "Arise and devour much flesh."

There is not much to go on here. I do not know the significance of being like a bear but I might be able to make a couple of inferences from being lifted up on one side and the three ribs in his mouth. The Meads and the Persians was, in the beginning, a kingdom of two peoples with two kings. However, one king was higher than the other. That would be Cyrus with Darius the Mead likely being the lower king. This is born out further in Daniel chapter 8 which we will get into in our next chapter. But the fact that one side of the bear was lifted higher than the other might be a reference to this. Granted that may be a stretch, and by itself not much to go on. But the three ribs in the mouth are also a clue and could represent the three major people groups conquered by this kingdom. These would be the Babylonians, Egypt and Lydia of Asia Minor. Again, it's not a lot to go on but of the five possible choices offered from Daniel 2, the kingdom of the Meads and the Persians is the one that comes closest to matching the symbols. And now we seem to be matching the chronology and timeline of the kingdoms given in Daniel 2.

The third beast is described in verse 6 as being like a leopard with four wings and four heads, and dominion was given to it. Since the first two seemed to be the gold and silver of the statue of Daniel 2, the question is, is there anything about the Brass kingdom, the Greek kingdom of Alexander the Great, which seems to fit with this beast of 4 wings and 4 heads. Well, yes, there is. We know from history (and we will see more about this in Daniel chapters 8 and 11) that Alexander had four generals that served under him. After Alexander's death these four generals competed and warred many years for the kingdom until they finally ended up dividing the kingdom between them. Again, it is a loose connection, but a connection, nonetheless, and has no closer match to any of the other kingdoms. Not to mention that once again it fits with the chronological timeline we learned from Daniel 2.

Finally, we come to the fourth beast which, if it follows suit, we would expect to represent the Roman kingdom. This beast is described in verse 7 as dreadful and terrible, exceeding strong, with iron teeth that devoured and broke things in pieces and stamped the residue with its feet. So far it seems to match with the Roman Empire nicely as it clearly was a very oppressive kingdom and the connection to the iron in the teeth is not lost.

But then the description seems to diverge from the fourth kingdom of Daniel 2 and starts to sound more like the fifth. The description goes on to say in verse 7 that this kingdom is "different" from the others *before* it and had ten horns. Being "different" was one of the characteristics of the fifth kingdom of iron and clay from Daniel 2. Also, the feet contained ten toes which coincide with the ten horns. And finally, the fifth kingdom also had the strength of the iron which would match with the iron teeth. But most importantly, this beast is destroyed by the kingdom of God as described in 7:11, which clearly ties it to the fifth kingdom of Daniel 2 which is destroyed by the Stone which is the Kingdom of God.

I also want to emphasize that little hint I gave above about our timeline that says that the first three kingdoms were *before* this fourth one. That at least limits the fourth kingdom of chapter 7 to the forth or fifth of chapter 2 because there has to be at least three kingdoms before it. But given the other clues, I would be inclined to say that the fourth kingdom of Daniel 7 matches with the fifth kingdom of Daniel 2 and the Roman kingdom of Daniel 2 is skipped in this chapter. It will be noted that this theme of skipping the Roman Kingdom is consistent throughout the rest of the prophecies of Daniel with only a slight ancillary mention in the historical narrative of Daniel 11:30 (ships of Chittim).

But let's go back now and look at what new information we can glean about this last kingdom of men starting in verse 8. We know this beast had ten horns and we know from verse 24 that these ten horns will be ten kings. In verse 8 this "little horn" plucked up three of the other horns by the roots. This tells me that there is instability or strife among the kings which also matches with the fifth kingdom of Daniel 2 where it says the kingdom will not be united.

This little horn has eyes and a mouth and speaks "great things." That doesn't mean "good" things. We know from verse 25 that it is referring to "great words against the most high." Though I'm jumping ahead a bit to things we will learn in Revelation, I believe this is our first introduction to the "man of sin" often referred to as the antichrist. Though there is nothing here in Daniel that says that, per say, I bring it up because I want to make an important distinction. Many who speak of end times are aware of a person that they refer to as the "antichrist." But in the same breath they often refer to him as "the beast." The distinction I would like to make here from Daniel 7 is that the little horn is not the beast. It is only part of the beast. The "beast" represents the kingdom. Or, if I may change the perspective a little bit, it represents a *political system.* The beast represents the *political system* of antichrist while the little horn represents the *man* antichrist. If you confuse the two, you will get a faulty picture from prophecies we will be studying later in Revelation.

So, even if we don't have enough solid clues in our study so far to claim that this little horn is indeed the "antichrist" commonly believed from Revelation, yet it is clear that he represents a king or ruler, just as the other horns represent kings or rulers, and that he will uproot three and rule over the final antichrist kingdom of men along with the other seven kings. Since this is an anti-kingdom of men which is of the spirit of antichrist and thus an antichrist political system that wants to rule the world, I do not find it uncomfortable to refer to this little horn as the "man" antichrist.

Verse 9 says Daniel beheld until the thrones were cast down. Many versions translate this to say the thrones were "set up." The Strong's definition of the word suggests more of a casting down but in any case it is not clear what this is about. Some think the thrones are set up and the Ancient of Days sits on one of them or some such thing. I am inclined to believe that this is a reference to the Ancient of Days overthrowing this last kingdom of men and casting down the thrones they were sitting on. But I make no bones about saying that is a guess.

Regardless of that, the description of the Ancient of Days, with a garment white as snow and hair as pure wool, a throne like fiery flame and *wheels* of burning fire, starts to sound like a vivid description of one who could only be the God of all. The wheels are a dead give away matching with the wheels as described by Ezekiel starting in Ezekiel 1:15. It goes on to say a fiery stream issued from before him and thousands and millions of beings stood before him. Pretty sure this is God the Father.

Then it says, "The judgment was set and the books were opened." (End of verse 10.) At this point we don't know what judgment this is or what the books are. But we will learn more about this in subsequent prophecies.

In verse 11 Daniel goes back and fills in some more details of what he had been seeing in the vision concerning the little horn. He said he was focused on him because of the great swelling words he spoke. Apparently, this guy will be a very powerful and charismatic speaker. Daniel watched until the *beast* was slain. It doesn't say the horn was slain, it says the beast was slain. The whole political system of antichrist will be slain, its body destroyed and given to the burning flame. I believe it can be safely assumed that the horns of the beast go with the body and are destroyed as well, but it is significant to note that not just the man antichrist is destroyed, but the whole political system. This is good news.

I should point out here that the "burning flame" is a new concept and is not explained here. At this point we don't know what that represents. I suspect it is the Lake of Fire described by Jesus in later passages and in Revelation, but for now I am content to just remember that the destruction of the beast is *by fire*. You will see this reference to fire at this point in the timeline again and again in prophecy.

It says in verse 12 that the rest of the beasts have their dominion or authority taken away but their lives were prolonged for a "season and a time." The literal translation of the word "season" would be about 3 months and the literal translation for "time" which in Hebrew means a "cycle" is usually a reference to a year. If I take this literally that would mean about 15 months. But I don't know if this is intended as literal or general and in the grand scheme of things I don't think it matters much. The one thing we can glean from this is that this "season and time" occurs after the judgment and the implication is that the lives of the beasts are forfeit beyond that. Keep in mind that the beasts represent political systems and not individual people. If I jump to the Maybe Box for just a moment, it could be that the governmental systems that are roughly in place throughout the world may be used temporarily while the transition to divine government is taking place. These systems would have no authority outside of Christ's divine authority and that of the redeemed that rule and reign with Him during the millennium, but perhaps used temporarily for the transition. That is *purely* speculation, however. Basically what I'm saying here is that we don't really know what verse 12 is talking about and to my knowledge it isn't explained anywhere else in the Bible. This, then, is one of those places where we don't know what the verse is talking about but it doesn't appear to make much difference to our understanding of the timeline so we'll just have to leave it as a mystery.

In verse 13 a new player on the scene is introduced. This would be "one like the son of man." We know from the gospels that Jesus often referred to himself as the son of man. Some believe he did this largely because of this verse in Daniel 7, attempting to link himself to this person in the vision. However, in the book of Ezekiel, God refers repeatedly to Ezekiel as "son of man." So Jesus' use of the term to refer to himself may or may not be significantly tied to this reference in Daniel. But, moving on, note that it says in Daniel he "came with the clouds of heaven." This theme of Jesus returning with the clouds of heaven should be remembered because it will show up time and time again in prophecy in our later studies.

So the son of man comes to the Ancient of Days and receives dominion and glory and a Kingdom that all people, nations and languages should serve him. (v.14) His dominion or authority is "everlasting" and "shall not pass away" and His Kingdom "shall not be destroyed." These descriptions clearly match with the sixth kingdom of Daniel 2 which speaks of the Kingdom of God, the Stone, being an everlasting Kingdom that will not be destroyed. (2:44).

Another interesting clue here in verse 14 is that the kingdom of this "son of man" will be served by *people, nations and languages.* This suggests to me that, whatever else will be in this Kingdom, there will at least be people, nations and languages. It implies rather strongly that there will be mortal men on the earth during Christ's earthly reign. We'll have to watch to see if this idea is confirmed later in other prophecies (which indeed it is.)

In verse 17 the angel begins to explain the vision. The first thing I notice is that the angel says the beasts shall arise out of the *earth* while Daniel said in verse 3 they arose from the *sea.* I don't know if there is any significance to this, but I noticed it. A good detective is always looking for clues. This may mean something to you, depending on your own experience or knowledge. For now, I'm content to note it and move on. I don't think it adds anything useful.

Verse 18 adds new information. "The saints of the most high shall take the kingdom and possess the kingdom for ever, even for ever and ever." It is interesting that the word "saints" is used here and not "Jews." The Hebrew word simply means "holy ones." But to the Jewish mentality of the time, *they* were the only holy ones. From our perspective in history, we know that Jews are no longer the only holy ones but that the Church of Jesus Christ would also be included under such a title. And it is interesting to note that the angel said "saints."

It also sounds like in the end we win. Ah, more good news. Since we know that this final Kingdom is a Kingdom of God, and the dominion is given to the Son of Man, and we (the holy ones) will also possess the Kingdom, it stands to reason that we will be together with the Son of Man ruling and reigning for ever and ever. This seems like a loose connection, but I emphasize it here because we will see this confirmed in later prophecies in Revelation 20.

Now in verse 19, Daniel begins to ask the angel about the fourth beast and the horns, etc. Here we find a new bit of information about this beast, which is that he has nails of brass. Again, I don't know the significance of that. If the iron teeth suggest a connection to the Romans, the brass nails would be a connection to the Greeks. But there is no other information in prophecy to confirm or refute those ideas. Obviously this kingdom will be strong and oppressive. At the very least we can gather that. Most likely the iron is just a reference to strength. And the brass...well, I don't know.

In verse 20 we get another little bit of information about the little horn. Though he began as a little horn with eyes and a mouth that spoke very great things, his "look was more stout than his fellows." The Hebrew word for "stout" actually refers to a captain or master or great lord. Thus I think the idea is that he will appear to be a great master or lord. He will look like a great captain or leader. I'm not sure exactly what that would look like. But when it happens we will remember these words were here and will be more likely to recognize it as a fulfillment of prophecy.

In verses 21 and 22 Daniel again goes back and shares more detail of the vision, describing now how this same horn makes war with the saints and *prevails against them!*" Yikes! Not so good news. This starts to sound like it could be a difficult time for the saints of the Most High. And note that so far in our study (Daniel 2 and Daniel 7) there has been no mention of "deliverance" for the saints or a massive catching away. Clearly this antichrist figure is going to hate the people of Christ and will begin a major campaign of persecution against them. In order for this to happen, the saints must be present. Well, at least it is nice we were made aware of this ahead of time so we can be emotionally and spiritually prepared. The time may be short. Are you ready for such a struggle? Now is the time to go deeper.

Verse 22 repeats what we learned in verses 11 and 18; that the Ancient of Days comes and judgment or dominion is given to the saints of the Most High, and the time comes that the saints possess the kingdom.

Now the angel, in verse 23 begins to give his answer. He says the forth beast shall be the fourth kingdom upon earth. This would suggest it should be the Roman kingdom but it is immediately followed by, "which shall be diverse (different) from all kingdoms" which doesn't fit the description of the Roman kingdom but of the future kingdom of iron and clay. Plus, all of these events concerning the ten kings and the one king plucking up three kings have no historical parallel in the history of the Roman Empire. Then you have the fact that the Stone strikes the kingdom of iron and clay, not the kingdom of iron in Daniel 2, and here in Daniel 7 the Ancient of Days slays the beast and gives him to the burning flame. These things just don't fit with the historical Roman kingdom. So, not withstanding the words of the angel at the beginning of verse 23, I don't believe this can be a reference to the Romans. It seems here, just as we will discover in subsequent prophecies of Daniel, that the Roman Empire is, for some reason, ignored. I have no explanation.

Some would seize upon this and try to claim that the explanation for this lies in the fact that the kingdom of iron and clay is simply a continuation of the Roman kingdom of iron. Well, in a sense that is true for each successive kingdom of man was (and will be) in many ways just a continuation of the one before it. But if you fail to differentiate between these two kingdoms or to recognize the future nature of the iron and clay kingdom, then you create many more conflicts with the writings than you solve. As we get into the latter chapters of Daniel where more and more detail is added to this prophetic picture of the kingdoms of men we will find again and again that the historical Roman Empire is completely ignored. I don't know why this is but I don't believe that it matters. And I would warn the reader not to try to make too much of this, or to try to use this to support the preconceived claim (which is really a speculation) that the future kingdom of iron and clay will somehow be a revived Roman Empire. More on this as we get to it.

In verse 24 the angel makes it plain that the ten horns are ten kings that shall arise and after them shall come another king that shall be *different* from the first ten. Again, I don't know exactly what that difference will be. We know he will "appear more stout" and that he will be quite an orator speaking many things against God. But I don't think we will fully understand this "difference" until we see it.

It also says in verse 24 that this new king will "subdue" three kings. The Hebrew word for "subdue" means to abase, humble or put down. It doesn't sound necessarily like a term of military defeat. Thus, I am inclined to think this is a political defeat rather than some sort of military defeat. I could be wrong, but jumping back for a moment to the Maybe Box, if the ten kings spoken of here are ten nations banding together to rule the whole world as some believe, then it would seem for this little king to defeat three of them it would have to be a massive military campaign. But if the world is being ruled by a committee of ten principle directors on a board and their power is only derived by agreements and treaties, then the path to power for the man antichrist would be a political battle, and not a military one. Though I believe we will find in later prophecies that there are indeed some military battles that will be fought during the time of this antichrist, the word "subdue" in relation to the defeat of these three kings seems to suggest a more political type defeat. But I cannot say that for sure just from this word.

In verse 25 the angel gives us more information about this man antichrist. He will speak great words against the Most High and shall wear out the saints of the Most High. Here is another reference to the great persecution of the saints as suggested in verse 21. "Wear out the saints," reminds me of the words of Jesus in Luke 21:19, "In your patience possess ye your souls."

Verse 25 also tells us that this man antichrist will change times and laws. Clearly he will see himself as a dictator that can change even the most fundamental aspects of world culture. I think this suggests he will attempt to alter the calendar much as was done by the Roman emperor Julius Caesar in 45 BC with the invention of the Julian calendar. At any rate, it could be that he will change the designations of weeks and months and years to something other than what we are used to, which may explain why in the prophecy here the angel says the saints will be given into his hand for a "time, times and the dividing of time." It could be there will be no more designation for a year or a month or a week. But this is just speculation.

At any rate, this phrase, "time, times and the dividing of time," we will learn later, represents a period of about three and one half years. The word "time" means "a cycle of time" in Hebrew but is defined by Strong's Concordance to also suggest a year. As for the term, "dividing of time" it may be a stretch to say it means "half" a cycle, but at least we can say it means a "part" of a cycle. Now for "times," the plural of "times" gives us no indication that it refers to just two. There is a "dual" form of plural in the Hebrew language which denotes a "pair" of something. But the dual form is not used here. The word "times" is just plural. So at the outset it would seem like a stretch to say this represents a period of three and one half years. However, there are prophecies that we will get to later that clearly identify the period as 42 months or 1260 days or even as we will see in Daniel 12, 1290 days, all of which come to about three and one half years. So, for now, even though it doesn't say it specifically in Daniel 7:25, I believe it is safe to say this represents three and one half years. For now I will just show it in the diagram below as a cycle, more than one cycle, and part of a cycle.

Finally, in verses 26 and 27 the judgment will sit which is a repeat of what we already know from verses earlier, and the dominion of that political system of antichrist will be taken away and he shall be destroyed *unto the end.* I'm not sure to the end of what. But at least it seems to be a reference to the end of the kingdoms of men. Since the Kingdom of God is an everlasting kingdom it cannot refer to the end of that. Perhaps it is a weak reference to the end of the millennial period, but that would be a stretch and a guess. (The thousand year millennial reign of Christ will be discussed in more detail in chapter 15 of this book.)

"And the Kingdom and dominion and the greatness of the kingdom under the whole heaven, shall be given to the people of the saints of the most high, whose kingdom is an everlasting kingdom and all dominions shall serve and obey him." There are a couple of hints we can get from this verse 27. This Kingdom that is referred to here is "under the whole heaven." I don't want to try to make too much of this, but this could be a weak reference to the millennial Kingdom which is Christ's thousand year reign on earth. We will learn in Revelation 20 that the saints of God are to rule and reign with Christ on the earth for a thousand years. This lines up very nicely with the descriptions given here in Daniel 7. Also, it becomes clear from this verse that the saints are to receive the kingdom right along with the Most High, which also nicely dovetails with Revelation 20 in saying we will be with Christ during this time ruling and reigning with him on the earth.

Ok, so now we have some hints for another timeline. It seems pretty clear that the first three beasts line up with the first three kingdoms of Daniel 2. Now we see an expansion of the last kingdom made of iron and clay. Here is a picture of how it would look.

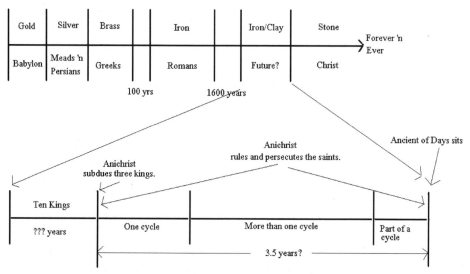

Figure 2: Expansion of the Last Kingdom of Men

So far we don't know how long the 10 kings will reign before the anti-king comes on the scene. Some suggest that the ten kings rule successively and not all at the same time which would suggest a long period of time. But the ten toes and ten horns are all there at the same time, and the fact that the man antichrist comes up "after" them (7:24) and then subdues three of them at once says pretty definitively that they all rule and reign at the same time. This will be reinforced by other prophecies in Revelation12, 13 and 17. For now, this is about all we can get from Daniel 7.

3. The Ram, the Goat and the Four Notable Ones: Daniel Chapter 8

Before studying this chapter, you should read Daniel, chapter 8.

Daniel chapter 8 opens in the third year of the reign of King Belshazzar. Belshazzar by historical accounts was the son of a guy named Nabonidus, but according to Daniel 5:22 he was the son of Nebuchadnezzar. Possibly he was the grandson of Nebuchadnezzar. At any rate, at the time of this vision he had been king in Babylon for three years. This occurred well before the "writing on the wall" event described in Daniel chapter 5.

Here Daniel receives yet another vision giving him another perspective on future events yet to come. In a nutshell, Daniel sees a ram with two horns, one horn being higher than the other. This ram was very powerful and conquered in all directions. Then came a he goat with a single "notable" horn that was more powerful than the ram and broke its two horns, cast him to the ground and stamped upon him. This goat grew very strong but the horn was suddenly broken and four "notable" horns came up in its place toward the four winds of heaven. Out of one of these horns came forth a "little horn" that became very great. This little horn causes the daily sacrifice to be taken away. Then one "saint" asks another in the vision "how long" will it be that the sanctuary is "trodden under foot." The answer is an exact number of days. After that a voice speaks to the archangel, Gabriel, to explain the vision to Daniel, which he does.

It is worthy to note that in this vision, much like the vision of chapter 7, there is no mention of the Roman kingdom of iron. As we will see below, the ram and the goat once again represent the kingdoms of silver and brass; the Medes and Persians and the Greeks. But then, as in chapter 7, it moves onto things that represent events and people in the last kingdom of iron and clay. The Roman kingdom of iron is not represented.

So let's go through this chapter in detail.

Starting in verse 3, Daniel sees a ram with two horns. The horns were high but one was higher than the other and came up after the first. This ram pushed westward, northward and southward so that no *beast* might stand before him, neither was there any that could deliver out of the ram's hand. The ram did according to his will and became great.

31

According to Gabriel, in verse 20, this ram represents the kings of Media and Persia. At the time Belshazzar was assassinated and the Medes and Persians took power there were two kings. The lesser king was Darius the Mede, who ruled from 559 BC to 539 BC, while the greater king or higher king was Cyrus of the Persians, who reigned from 559 BC to 529 BC. That explains the horns of the ram with one being higher than the other. Also, this would match with the bear in Daniel chapter 7, which stood up on one side and thus was higher on one side than the other.

Just for historical information, the greatest king of the Meads and Persians, who reigned from 485 BC to 464 BC, was Xerxes. Following Xerxes the kingdom gradually declined. It should be noted that Xerxes invaded Greece during his reign and committed many atrocities which planted into the hearts of the Grecian people a deep hatred for the Medes and Persians. This hatred was passed down to later generations and became one of the formative attitudes of Alexander the Great. I'll say more on this later in this chapter and in our study of Daniel chapter 11.

Now in verse 5, Daniel sees a he goat coming from the west "on the face of the whole earth" that touched not the ground and had a notable horn between his eyes. According to Gabriel, in verse 21, this he goat is Greece and the notable horn is the first king, which would be Alexander the Great. Greece is to the West of the area controlled by the Meads and Persians. The goat was "on the face of the whole earth" which might suggest the size of his army, and he "touched not the ground" which might suggest how fast his movements were. This same theme of speed is suggested by the "four wings" of the leopard of Daniel chapter 7, which also adds credence to the belief that the leopard of Daniel 7 is also Greece.

In verses 6, 7 and 8 this goat comes to the ram and runs at him in the fury of his power. He is moved with "choler" which is intense anger, which came, no doubt, from his prejudiced hatred of the Medes and Persians passed down to him from his parents. The goat breaks the horns of the ram and stamps him underfoot, which, of course, Alexander did when he defeated the Medes and Persians in 330 BC. "When he was strong the great horn was broken." Alexander conquered many lands in his short reign but died suddenly at the young age of 32. Some believe it was by poisoning. "...and for it [the one horn] came up four notable ones [horns] toward the four winds of heaven." After his death there was a series of battles fought over who would take his throne, which eventually resulted in the kingdom being divided among his four generals. Following are excerpts from a Wikipedia article giving greater detail on Alexander the Great.

Alexander III of Macedon (356–323 BC), popularly known as **Alexander the Great** (Greek: Μέγας Ἀλέξανδρος, *Mégas Aléxandros*), was a Greek king (basileus) of Macedon. He is the most celebrated member of the Argead Dynasty and created one of the largest empires in ancient history. Born in Pella in 356 BC, Alexander was tutored by the famed philosopher Aristotle, succeeded his father Philip II of Macedon to the throne in 336 BC after the King was assassinated and died thirteen years later at the age of 32. Although both Alexander's reign and empire were short-lived, the cultural impact of his conquests lasted for centuries. Alexander was known to be undefeated in battle and is considered one of the most successful commanders of all time. He is one of the most famous figures of antiquity, and is remembered for his tactical ability, his conquests, and for spreading Greek culture into the East (marking the beginning of Hellenistic civilization).

Philip had brought most of the city-states of mainland Greece under Macedonian hegemony, using both military and diplomatic means. Upon Philip's death, Alexander inherited a strong kingdom and an experienced army. He succeeded in being awarded the generalship of Greece and, with his authority firmly established, launched the military plans for expansion left by his father. He invaded Persian-ruled Asia Minor, and began a series of campaigns lasting ten years. Alexander repeatedly defeated the Persians in battle; marched through Syria, Egypt, Mesopotamia, Persia, and Bactria; and in the process he overthrew the Persian king Darius III and conquered the entirety of the Persian Empire. Following his desire to reach the "ends of the world and the Great Outer Sea", he invaded India, but was eventually forced to turn back by the near-mutiny of his troops.

Alexander died in Babylon in 323 BC, before realizing a series of planned campaigns that would have begun with an invasion of Arabia. In the years following Alexander's death, a series of civil wars tore his empire apart, which resulted in the formation of a number of states ruled by Macedonian aristocracy (the Diadochi). Remarkable though his conquests were, Alexander's lasting legacy was not his reign, but the cultural diffusion in his conquests engendered. Alexander's importation of Greek colonists and culture to the East resulted in a new *Hellenistic* culture, aspects of which were still evident in the traditions of the Byzantine Empire until the mid-15th century. Alexander became legendary as a classical hero in the mold of Achilles, and features prominently in the history and myth of Greek and non-Greek cultures. He became the measure against which generals, even to this day, compare themselves, and military academies throughout the world still teach his tactical exploits.

Division of the Empire

Alexander had no obvious or legitimate heir, his son Alexander IV by Roxane being born after Alexander's death. This left the huge question as to who would rule the newly conquered, and barely pacified Empire. According to Diodorus, Alexander's companions asked him when he was on his deathbed to whom he bequeathed his kingdom; his laconic reply was "tôi kratistôi"—"to the strongest". Given that Arrian and Plutarch have Alexander speechless by this point, it is possible that this is an apocryphal story. Diodorus, Curtius and Justin also have the more plausible story of Alexander passing his signet ring to Perdiccas, one of his bodyguards and leader of the companion cavalry, in front of witnesses, thereby possibly nominating Perdiccas as his successor.

In any event, Perdiccas initially avoided explicitly claiming power, instead suggesting that Roxane's baby would be king, if male; with himself, Craterus, Leonnatus and Antipater as guardians. However, the infantry, under the command of Meleager, rejected this arrangement since they had been excluded from the discussion. Instead, they supported Alexander's half-brother Philip Arrhidaeus. Eventually, the two sides reconciled, and after the birth of Alexander IV, he and Philip III were appointed joint kings of the Empire—albeit in name only.

It was not long, however, before dissension and rivalry began to afflict the Macedonians. The satrapies handed out by Perdiccas at the Partition of Babylon became power bases each general could use to launch his own bid for power. After the assassination of Perdiccas in 321 BC, all semblance of Macedonian unity collapsed, and 40 years of war between "The Successors" (*Diadochi*) ensued before the Hellenistic world settled into four stable power blocks: the Ptolemaic kingdom of Egypt, the Seleucid Empire in the east, the Kingdom of Pergamon in Asia Minor, and Macedon. In the process, both Alexander IV and Philip III were murdered.

Verse 9, "And out of one of them [one of the four horns] came forth a little horn…" Once again we see the "little horn" rising up out of the other horns. This is very reminiscent of the "little horn" of Daniel 7. Even the descriptions of the horn here and in verses 23-25 from Gabriel sound similar to those of the little horn of Daniel 7. But here the little horn represents a historical figure, Antiochus Epiphanies, who came to power over the Seleucid quarter of the Greek empire in 175 BC.

According to verses 9 through 12, this little horn waxed very great toward the South and toward the East and toward the pleasant land, which would be Israel. He waxed great even to the "host of heaven and it cast down some of the host and of the stars to the ground, and stamped upon them." Antiochus Epiphanies was ruthless and put to death many of the Jews including the priests of the temple. "He magnified himself even to the prince of the host and by him the daily sacrifice was taken away…" Antiochus killed the high priest and in a bid to destroy the Jewish traditions and worship and to install his own Greek culture, he took away their daily sacrifices and had pigs sacrificed on the altar of God to desecrate it. Following are excerpts from a Wikipedia article giving more detail on Antiochus Epiphanies.

> **Antiochus IV Epiphanes** ("**Manifest (God)**", "**the Illustrious**"; from Greek: Ἀντίοχος Ἐπιφανὴς; born c. 215 BC; died 164 BC) ruled the Seleucid Empire from 175 BC until his death in 164 BC. He was a son of King Antiochus III the Great and the brother of Seleucus IV Philopator. His original name was Mithridates; he assumed the name Antiochus after he assumed the throne.
>
> Notable events during the reign of Antiochus IV include his near-conquest of Egypt, which led to a confrontation that became an origin of the metaphorical phrase, "line in the sand" (see below), and the rebellion of the Jewish Maccabees.
>
> He assumed divine epithets, which no other Hellenistic king had done, such as *Theos Epiphanes* (Greek: *ΘΕΟΣ ΕΠΙΦΑΝΗΣ* mean "God Manifest") and after his defeat of Egypt, *Nikephoros* (Greek: *ΝΙΚΗΦΟΡΟΣ* mean "Bearer of Victory") But his often eccentric behavior, capricious actions and even insanity led some of his contemporaries to call him *Epimanes* ("The Mad One"), a word play on his title *Epiphanes*.

Rise to Power

As the son and a potential successor of King Antiochus III, Antiochus became a political hostage of the Roman Republic following the Peace of Apamea in 188 BC. When his older brother, Seleucus IV followed his father onto the throne in 187 BC, Antiochus was exchanged for his nephew Demetrius I Soter (the son and heir of Seleucus). After King Seleucus was assassinated by Heliodorus, a usurper, in 175 BC, Antiochus in turn ousted him. Since Seleucus' true heir, Demetrius I Soter, was still a hostage in Rome, Antiochus, with the help of King Eumenes II of Pergamum, seized the throne for himself, proclaiming himself co-regent for another son of Seleucus, an infant named Antiochus (whom he then murdered a few years later).

Wars against Egypt

When the guardians of King Ptolemy VI of Egypt demanded the return of Coele-Syria in 170 BC, Antiochus launched a preemptive strike against Egypt, conquering all but Alexandria and capturing King Ptolemy. To avoid alarming Rome, Antiochus allowed Ptolemy VI to continue ruling as a Puppet-king. Upon Antiochus' withdrawal, the city of Alexandria chose a new King, one of Ptolemy's brothers, also named Ptolemy (VIII Euergetes). Instead of fighting a civil war, the Ptolemy brothers agreed to rule Egypt jointly.

In 168 BC Antiochus led a second attack on Egypt and also sent a fleet to capture Cyprus. Before reaching Alexandria, his path was blocked by a single, old Roman ambassador named Gaius Popillius Laenas, who delivered a message from the Roman Senate directing Antiochus to withdraw his armies from Egypt and Cyprus, or consider themselves in a state of war with the Roman Republic. Antiochus said he would discuss it with his council, whereupon the Roman envoy drew a line in the sand around him and said, "Before you cross this circle I want you to give me a reply for the Roman Senate" - implying that Rome would declare war if the King stepped out of the circle without committing to leave Egypt immediately. Weighing his options, Antiochus wisely decided to withdraw. Only then did Popillius agree to shake hands with him.

Sacking of Jerusalem and Persecution of Jews

While Antiochus was busy in Egypt, a false rumor spread that he had been killed. The deposed High Priest Jason gathered a force of 1,000 soldiers and made a surprise attack on the city of Jerusalem. An official

Antiochus appointed as High Priest, Menelaus, was forced to flee Jerusalem during a riot. On the King's return from Egypt in 167 BC enraged by his defeat, he attacked Jerusalem and restored Menelaus, then executed many Jews.

2 Maccabees 5:11-14

When these happenings were reported to the king, he thought that Judea was in revolt. Raging like a wild animal, he set out from Egypt and took Jerusalem by storm. He ordered his soldiers to cut down without mercy those whom they met and to slay those who took refuge in their houses. There was a massacre of young and old, a killing of women and children, a slaughter of virgins and infants. In the space of three days, eighty thousand were lost, forty thousand meeting a violent death, and the same number being sold into slavery.

To consolidate his empire and strengthen his hold over the region, Antiochus decided to side with the Hellenized Jews by outlawing Jewish religious rites and traditions observed by more orthodox Jews and by ordering the worship of Zeus as the supreme god. This was anathema to the Jews and when they refused, Antiochus sent an army to enforce his decree. Because of the resistance, the city was destroyed, many were slaughtered, and a military Greek citadel called the Acra was established.

2 Maccabees 6:1-11

Not long after this the king sent an Athenian senator to force the Jews to abandon the customs of their ancestors and live no longer by the laws of God; also to profane the temple in Jerusalem and dedicate it to Olympian Zeus, and that on Mount Gerizim to Zeus the Hospitable, as the inhabitants of the place requested...They also brought into the temple things that were forbidden, so that the altar was covered with abominable offerings prohibited by the laws. A man could not keep the sabbath or celebrate the traditional feasts, nor even admit that he was a Jew. At the suggestion of the citizens of Ptolemais, a decree was issued ordering the neighboring Greek cities to act in the same way against the Jews: oblige them to partake of the sacrifices, and put to death those who would not consent to adopt the customs of the Greeks. It was obvious, therefore, that disaster impended. Thus, two women who were arrested for having circumcised their children were publicly paraded about the city with their babies hanging at their breasts and then thrown down from the top of the city wall. Others, who had assembled in nearby caves to observe the sabbath in secret, were betrayed to Philip and all burned to death.

Rebellion of the Maccabees

Most modern scholars argue that the king was in fact intervening in an internal civil war between the traditionalist Jews in the country and the Hellenized Jews in Jerusalem. According to Joseph P. Schultz:

Modern scholarship on the other hand considers the Maccabean revolt less as an uprising against foreign oppression than as a civil war between the orthodox and reformist parties in the Jewish camp.

These competed violently over who would be the High Priest, with traditionalists with Hebrew/Aramaic names like Onias contesting with Hellenizers with Greek names like Jason and Menelaus. Other authors point to possible socio/economic motives in addition to the religious motives behind the civil war.

What began in many respects as a civil war escalated when the Hellenistic kingdom of Syria sided with the Hellenizing Jews in their conflict with the traditionalists. As the conflict escalated, Antiochus took the side of the Hellenizers by prohibiting the religious practices the traditionalists had rallied around. This may explain why the king, in a total departure from Seleucid practice in all other places and times, banned the traditional religion of a whole people.

Final years

Taking advantage of Antiochus' western problems, King Mithridates I of Parthia attacked from the east and seized the city of Herat in 167 BC, disrupting the direct trade route to India and effectively splitting the Greek world in two.

Recognizing the potential danger in the east, but unwilling to give up control of Judea, Antiochus sent a commander named Lysias to deal with the Maccabees, while the King himself led the main Seleucid army against the Parthians. After initial success in his eastern campaign, including the reoccupation of Armenia, Antiochus died suddenly of disease in 164 BC.

I'll have more on the history of this man from Daniel chapter 11.

Verses 13 and 14: In the vision Daniel hears one "saint" speak to another and ask, "How long shall be the vision concerning the daily sacrifice and the transgression of desolation, to give both the sanctuary and the host to be trodden under foot?" The answer in verse 14 is, "Unto two thousand and three hundred *days*, then shall the sanctuary be cleansed."

The word "days" is used in the King James Bible, but the original Hebrew here does not say days, but rather says *evenings and mornings*. This makes a dramatic difference; for if you calculate two thousand three hundred days, this comes to about 6.4 years. But if you calculate two thousand three hundred evenings and mornings, this would equal only one thousand one hundred and fifty days, which comes to about 3.2 years. As it turns out, it was exactly 3.2 years after Antiochus defiled the altar and the temple (168 BC) before it was retaken by the Maccabees and cleansed in 165 BC. Thus history confirms the accuracy of the use of "evenings and mornings," counting each as one, rather than the translated "days."

As we work through these historical accounts of Antiochus Epiphanies it is noteworthy to see how they parallel with future accounts of the man antichrist. Already we have seen in Daniel chapter 7 that the "little horn," after he comes to power, makes war with the saints for a period that appears to work out to 3.5 years. Antiochus also made war with the people of God, the Jews, and destroyed the "host of heaven" and desecrated the temple with what will come to be known as the "abomination of desolation" which puts an end to the daily sacrifice. This lasts for about 3.2 years before it is cleansed and the daily sacrifice is again restarted.

Now Gabriel goes on and gives more detail concerning this vision. But pay attention to certain phrases that seem to place the significance of the vision at the "time of the end" rather than just somewhere in the stream of history.

In verse 17 Gabriel said, "Understand, O son of man: for *at the time of the end* shall be the vision." [emphasis mine] "…at the time of the end…" At the end of what? The antics of Antiochus in desecrating the temple did not represent the end of Jewish history or the end of any particular era. The desecration lasted less than three and a half years before the daily

39

sacrifice was again restarted and Jewish history went on its merry way. The time period of Antiochus Epiphanies does not represent the end of anything. So what is Gabriel referring to here? Again, in verse 19 Gabriel says, "Behold, I will make thee know what shall be in *the last end of the indignation*: for at the time appointed *the end shall be.*" [emphasis mine] "…the end shall be…" Again, I ask, the end of what? Also in here Gabriel uses the phrase, "…*last* end…" which suggests there is no later end to the "indignation." If this is the last one, there can be no other to come. But there are prophecies we have yet to look at that make it clear there is another time of "indignation" that is even today yet to come. Then at the end of verse 25 he says, "…he shall also stand up against the Prince of princes…" The only "Prince of princes" I know of is Jesus and there is no historical person by which we can connect this claim to the historical Antiochus. These statements taken together seem to be saying that the prophecies in the latter part of this chapter, though at first glance seeming to be about Antiochus, are parallel prophecies that would be more properly applied to the man antichrist. Additional prophecies in the gospels and in Revelation will show us that this assumption is not a stretch.

Now verses 20 through 22 are clearly historical for Gabriel explains them unquestionably as pictures of the Medes and Persians, the Greeks and Alexander the Great. It is also clear that in verse 23 Gabriel is beginning by referring to Antiochus Epiphanies. However, from here through verse 25 and from verses 9-14 we begin to see things that parallel not only what we already know about the man antichrist, but things we will also discover in later prophecies about him.

Based on what we know now, let's take a look at the parallels between the vision of chapter 7, which is clearly about the last kingdom of iron and clay and the man antichrist, and the vision of chapter 8.

> 7:8 A little horn comes up among the ten horns.
> 8:9 A little horn comes forth from among the four horns.
> ----------
> 7:8, 11, 25 The little horn has a mouth speaking great things against the most high and thinks to change times and laws.
> 8:11-12, 23-25 The little horn shall magnify himself (11), cast down the truth (12) shall understand dark sentences (riddles or proverbs) (23) his power shall not be by his own power (thus by

Satan's) (24) and shall cause craft (deceit) to prosper in his hand and shall magnify himself in his heart (25).

7:9   The "beast had great iron teeth and brass claws and was exceeding dreadful and devoured, brake in pieces and stamped the residue with his feet. An oppressive government.
8:24   A king whose power shall be mighty and shall destroy wonderfully.

7:21, 25   The horn will make war with the saints and prevail against them (21). He will wear out the saints (25).
8:24   The horn shall destroy the mighty and the holy people.

7:20   His look was more stout than his fellows.
8:23   A king of fierce countenance shall stand up.

7:11, 22, 26   The beast (along with the horn) is slain and cast in the fire (11, 22) by the Ancient of Days. The judgment shall sit and they shall take away his dominion (26).
8:25   The horn shall go against the prince of princes but shall be broken without hand (by God and not by the hands of men.)

7:25   They shall be given into his hand for a time, times and the dividing of time.
8:14   Unto 2,300 evenings and mornings (3.2 years): then shall the sanctuary be cleansed.

So here we are. There will be a future kingdom of man, a political system of antichrist, which will rule the whole earth. This kingdom will be initially led by ten kings. It will be strong as iron and oppressive but also broken and fragile. The peoples of this kingdom will mingle and intermarry but they will not become one people. They will not cling to each other but shall remain divided. At some time, another king will arise who shall be a great orator, speaking great things. He will come to power ruthlessly by uprooting three kings and destroying wonderfully. He will be a man of fierce countenance whose looks are "more stout" than his fellows. He will be a king who speaks great swelling words against God and who gets his great power from Satan. He will also cause craft, which is deceit, to prosper, understanding dark riddles and sentences. He will hate the mighty and the holy people making war with the saints and prevailing against them with a great persecution. This will continue for a time, times and the dividing of time until the Ancient of Days sits and the Son of Man comes in judgment. They will come with the saints of God to destroy this man and his antichrist political system by fire and to establish the Kingdom of God which shall never be destroyed, and shall be ruled by the Son of Man and his saints forever. Part of that Kingdom shall be here on earth with peoples and nations and languages, in other words mortals, still living on the planet.

None of this is speculation or comes from stretching or exaggeration of texts. All of this is straight from the writings of prophecy. And we have just begun.

4. The Seventy Weeks of Daniel Chapter 9

Before studying this chapter, you should read Daniel, Chapter 9.

Chapter 9 is one of the most fascinating chapters in Daniel and one that has created many theories and controversies. I won't spend much time on most of the various theories because the proponents of these theories ignore the plain statements of prophecy to make their theories work and thus in my view invalidate themselves. But I will touch on a few of them. And I believe it will become clear as we work through this that these theories require too much stretching and molding and isolation of scripture to be believed.

The meat of chapter 9 starts in verse 24 but before we go there I want to point out something in verse 4. Note the phrase, "...the great and dreadful God, keeping *the covenant*...." (הַבְּרִית) This term "the covenant" refers to the covenant of Israel which God made with Abraham and with Moses. This term will be used again in verse 27 where it is not as immediately obvious that it refers to Israel's old covenant. But it is important to keep this in mind. This term is also used several times in chapter 11. I'll discuss this in more detail when we get to verse 9:27.

But for now, let's start with verse 24. "Seventy weeks are determined upon thy people and upon thy Holy City..." Literally in Hebrew it says, "seventy sevens." It is generally considered to be without question that the angel was talking here about weeks of years because of the context of the verses that follow and because of how accurately it calculates to the events of Messiah that are now history. There are those that attempt to refute this but those theories are not worth examining here because they are easily refuted and a waste of space. If you run into them just pay attention to their use of scripture "isolation," which is ignoring the larger body of writings that contradict their claim, and "stretching" which is to make words mean something more than what they say.

Seventy sevens of years would be 490 years. It is also important to note here that Gabriel says these "weeks" of years are determined "upon thy people." That would seem to say that this vision concerns particularly the Jewish people. Though many end times prophecies, such as the earlier ones in Daniel, clearly involve the church and the "saints" of God, yet this

43

one seems to be concerned with a number of years that are determined for the people of Israel. So the angel is saying that God has determined there will be yet only 490 years of *significant* history for Daniel's people, the Jews.

This period, according to verse 24, is to "finish the transgression, and to make an end to sins, and to make reconciliation for iniquity, and to bring in everlasting righteousness, and to seal up the vision and prophecy, and to anoint the most Holy." I do not know specifically what event each of these things refers to, but most seem to be clear references to the work of Jesus. To put an end to sin and make reconciliation for iniquity sounds like the work of the cross. Finish the transgression, bring in everlasting righteousness and anoint the most Holy seem to refer to the establishment of the Kingdom of Jesus at the beginning of the millennium. If this is indeed a reference to the millennial kingdom, then this would equate the end of the seventy weeks with the return of Christ and the beginning of his Kingdom on earth. I don't know what is meant by the sealing of the vision and prophecy, but it could be a reference to the end of the Old Testament prophecy era which ended with Malachi around 397 BC, or it could mean the fulfillment of all visions and prophecy, or it could mean something else entirely. For our purposes, I don't think it matters whether or not we know for sure what this means and it does not give us much help with our timeline.

Verse 25 adds more detail. "…from the going forth of the commandment to restore and to build Jerusalem unto the Messiah the Prince shall be seven weeks and threescore and two weeks." Also, in verse 26 it says, "And after three score and two weeks shall Messiah be cut off…" So apparently, sixty nine of the 70 weeks, which is a span of 483 years, should take us to the time of Jesus' death. We can look at this from a couple of directions. We can calculate backwards from Jesus' death which is believed to be around 33 AD and see what date we find, or we can look for when the commandment to restore and rebuild Jerusalem went out and calculate forward to see if we come to around 33 AD, the believed time of the death of Jesus. We shall do it both ways.

But before we do this, we first have to do some conversions. The Jewish year at that time was considered to be 360 days long, not 365 days like ours. Because of their short year, the Hebrews had to add a month to their calendar every six or seven years to keep it in sync with the solar year.

The same is true today. But this is not taken into account here in this prophecy. So to convert this prophesied time period into solar years, we have to do some math. 483 Hebrew years at 360 days a year would equate to 173,880 days. The solar year is 365.25 days. So if we divide 173,880 by 365.25 we get 476 solar years. If we subtract 476 years from 33 AD we get 443 BC. But when BC changes to AD on the calendar there is no year 0, so we have to go one more year to get 444 BC. Well, this date falls on or about the 20th year of the reign of Artaxerxes of the Medes and Persians. That is very interesting because if you look in Nehemiah 2:1-6 you find that in the twentieth year of the reign of Artaxerxes it, "...pleased the king to send me [Nehemiah]..." to rebuild the city of Jerusalem. So, here is the commandment to rebuild the city as prophesied in verse 25. And exactly 476 solar years later, Jesus is crucified. This gives a lot of credibility to the common belief that Jesus was crucified in 33 AD.

Daniel 7:25 says during the time of those weeks of years, "...the street shall be built again and the wall even in troublous times." If you read the whole account in the book of Nehemiah, you will read of the story of how the wall of the city was rebuilt in 52 days (Nehemiah 6:15) during a time of resistance from the local people; exactly as Daniel prophesied.

But this period of sixty nine weeks is broken up into two segments, one being 7 weeks (of years) and one being 62 weeks. We know where 69 weeks take us but where does the 7 weeks take us? Seven weeks of years would be 49 years. 49 times 360 days equals 17,640 days. Divide that by 365.25 days in the solar year and you get 48.3 solar years. Starting once again from 444 BC this takes us up to 395.7 BC or about 396 BC. What happened in 396 BC? It just so happens that this marks the end of the period of Old Testament revelation as the last prophet, Malachi, ends his ministry. History records this as being in 397 BC which, given the uncertainty of the exact dates of Artaxerxes' reign and the death of Christ, not to mention when Malachi's ministry may have actually ended, is well in range to be considered accurate; one year.

So it appears the vision was saying to Daniel, there will be 48 years to the end of the period of the prophets of the Old Testament, which may be a reference back to 9:24, "...to seal up the vision and prophecy...", and 476 years to the death of Messiah, starting from the time the commandment will go forth to rebuilt the city of Jerusalem. That's exactly what happened. It's all pretty simple and pretty plain.

Now, just for completeness, there are some theories that try to fit this prophecy into other periods of history and attempt to make them fit by calculating them from other significant dates, such as the command that went fort to rebuild the *temple* in Jerusalem. This actually happened some 92 years before the command to rebuild the city when, according to Ezra 1, Cyrus king of Persia, in his first year, which was around 536 BC, was stirred up by God to cause the temple of God to be rebuilt in Jerusalem. So he commanded it to be so. The book of Ezra is all about this history. It took about 21 years to build the temple and it was finished (Ezra 6:15) in the sixth year of Darius the First (not to be confused with Darius the Meade), which was about 515 BC. Trying to run the numbers from this date (536 BC) simply does not work for anything but there are those that try to make something of it by adding gaps or massaging the information around to try to make it fit. Others try to start the time from the beginning of the captivity in 588 BC, because they try to put all 70 weeks together as one period of 483 solar years and make it come out to the cleansing of the temple by the Maccabeus in 165 BC. This only comes to 423 years, but who's counting? If you try to squeeze the date back to the first carrying away into captivity in 603 BC, you get up to 438 years. But that's still short of 483.

I'm not sure why anyone wants to try to squeeze the 70 weeks of Daniel chapter 9 into some other point in history when there is no question as to when it was to start and how it calculates precisely to the times spoken of in Daniel 9. Perhaps it is because the obvious interpretation messes up some other theory or doctrine they hold concerning end times. I don't know. But some people are just not satisfied with the plain bald face truth of the prophecies. I only mention these other views because you will, no doubt, run into them if you read other studies on Daniel 9.

It says in verse 26, "And after threescore and two weeks shall Messiah be cut off, but not for himself, and the people of the prince that shall come shall destroy the city and the sanctuary and the end thereof shall be with a flood and unto the end of the war desolations are determined." So this says the temple and the sanctuary are going to be destroyed. Well, that did happen in 70 AD, 37 years after the crucifixion, when Titus the Roman attacked the city and destroyed it, burning the temple. The Hebrew word for "flood" can also mean a "flow," or, "fluency." There was no literal flood of water during the destruction of Jerusalem and the temple.

Therefore, this is most likely a reference to the overflowing Roman army that overwhelmed the city of Jerusalem.

But then we get to an intriguing text in verse 27. It says, "And he shall confirm the covenant with many for one week: and in the midst of the week he shall cause the sacrifice and the oblation to cease." This one verse is at the center of many controversies, crazy ideas and theories and at first glance seems to be out of place. Clearly this is an explanation of the 70th week with the words, "…he shall confirm the covenant with many for *one week*." But then it talks about the sacrifice and oblation ceasing. How can the sacrifices cease if there is no temple for them to be happening in? The temple was destroyed in verse 26. Is the chronology off here? And who is the "he?" Does it refer to the Messiah, the people of the prince to come or the prince to come himself? Who is this prince? Is he the man antichrist? And what is the covenant? Is it a seven year peace treaty as so many claim? If so, with whom? There are lots of good questions here and I'll address them all below. But first let's examine one of the more common theories proposed to explain these verses.

There is a theory out there that agrees with the numbers and dates I've mentioned above for the 69 weeks, but then tries to suggest that the last week of years occurred right after the sixty ninth week in history. In other words, that all 490 years are congruent, connected and continuous. At first thought this would seem to make sense, but when you look at the texts of verse closely the logic begins to break down. This theory supposes that Jesus, himself, fulfilled the last week and that the Messiah is, in fact, the "he" referred to in verse 27 that confirms covenant and stops the sacrifices. Jesus' ministry is said in this theory to have lasted about three and a half years. Most scholars say it was only three years, but this theory stretches that a bit to make it work. So Jesus ministered for three and a half years and then was crucified. With the death of the Messiah, the way of salvation by faith was paved and this put an end to the sacrifice and oblation as God's way of salvation. In other words, the theory says that with Jesus' death the Old Testament law is no longer valid and the New Testament of faith is now in force. Thus the sacrifices and oblations no longer have meaning or purpose and essentially "ended." Then, supposedly, Jesus continued to minister in his glorified body for another three and a half years on the earth, thus fulfilling the 70th week. Here are the problems with this idea.

The prophecy says it is 62 weeks (after the first 7 weeks) until Messiah is cut off. This theory would require the time to be sixty two and a half weeks because Jesus was still alive, according to them, for the first half of the last week. They would argue that verse 26 says "after" the sixty two weeks he is cut off and thus it doesn't have to be precise. The middle of the last week is "after" the end of the sixty two. Ok, but now we're starting to manipulate things to make the theory work. Also, this means the crucifixion of Jesus would calculate to 36.5 AD. Given the ambiguity of the dates, this is still within the margin of error, but we are pulling at it.

Now the idea that his death caused the sacrifice and oblation to cease is also problematic. In reality the sacrifice and oblation continued for an additional 37 or so years until the Romans destroyed the temple in 70 AD. So to counter that, they suggest that this was a spiritual ending since the death of Christ marked the end of the usefulness of the law and the beginning of salvation by faith. He was the last sacrifice. I get the significance of that, but on a spiritual level, no one was ever saved or justified by the blood of bulls and goats (Heb. 10:4). Salvation and the forgiveness of sins have *always* been by faith. And there is nothing in this verse of Daniel 9:27 to suggest he is talking about some spiritual ceasing of the significance of the sacrifice. The words seem to quite clearly speak of the literal ceasing of the sacrifice. This is further strengthened by the parallel prophecies of Daniel 8 where Antiochus Epiphanies literally ended the sacrifices. And the fact remains that the daily sacrifice continued long after Jesus was crucified. So I'd say they are really reaching and "spiritualizing" the text to make this one work.

Then when it comes to the end of the seven years, they are suggesting that Jesus' ministry continued on the earth for three and a half years after he rose from the dead. It is true he did minister on earth for a time by appearing to many. However there is no record of how long this went on or when it ceased. This theory places an artificial end date of 3.5 years after Jesus' crucifixion to the end of his ministry on earth. There is no recorded event to mark this end to the 70 weeks of years. It just sort of hangs out there.

But along these lines, the prophecy suggests that these 70 weeks of years mark the completion of significant Jewish history. The angel was saying in essence, "This is all that is allotted to your people." Now if you back up and attempt to use the crucifixion of Christ as the event that marks the end of significant Jewish history at 33 AD, then you must say that the 70th week of years somehow overlaps the 62 weeks, or it pushes the date of the crucifixion out to 40 AD and there is no significant event to mark the *beginning* of that last seven years. But if you hold to the original theory discussed above then all of significant Jewish history ended three and a half years after the crucifixion and there is no event recorded in history to mark its passing.

In my view, all of this is fruitless wasted effort, trying to justify some other false belief by attempting to explain away obvious truth. The fact is, the sacrifices continued after the death of Christ for some 37 years until the temple was destroyed in 70 AD. There has never been a temple or daily sacrifice since. The words of this prophecy have never been fulfilled. Therefore, this last seven year period *must* be future.

So what are verses 26 and 27 really saying? Do they make sense or not? I really struggled with these questions because verse 27 does not flow well grammatically (in English) from verse 26. I often wondered if a verse was missing, as has been suggested by others, or if something was mistranslated. It just didn't make good sense. The only way to solve this was to go deeper into the original Hebrew. So that's what I did.

Just so you know, I began my research into the Hebrew language long before I began this project. I have studied Hebrew for many years. I am by no means a scholar in the language, nor am I fluent. But I have learned quite a bit. Hebrew is a very complex language but does have consistent rules of grammar that once learned give the reader great insight into what is being communicated. The first thing you have to learn is that every word in Hebrew is either masculine or feminine or both. There is no neuter in Hebrew, no "it."

So, I'm going to go over these two verses in detail. The following discussion of Hebrew verbs and grammar may appear a bit technical and overwhelming at first, but I believe I can break it down for those who have no experience with the language and I'll summarize what I've discovered at the end of the discussion. To begin, I'm going to show the actual Hebrew (which reads from right to left.) Then I will show the text paralleled with a literal translation in English on the line below it. Then I will discuss what's going on grammatically in the paragraphs following. Here we go:

49

Daniel 9:26:

וְאַחֲרֵי הַשָּׁבֻעִים שִׁשִּׁים וּשְׁנַיִם יִכָּרֵת מָשִׁיחַ וְאֵין לוֹ
וְהָעִיר וְהַקֹּדֶשׁ יַשְׁחִית עַם נָגִיד הַבָּא וְקִצּוֹ בַשֶּׁטֶף וְעַד קֵץ
מִלְחָמָה נֶחֱרֶצֶת שֹׁמֵמוֹת :

Now the parallel translation:

וְאַחֲרֵי   הַשָּׁבֻעִים   שִׁשִּׁים   וּשְׁנַיִם   יִכָּרֵת   מָשִׁיחַ   וְאֵין לוֹ
(for him) (but not) (Messiah) (he shall be cut off) (and two) (sixty) (the sevens) (And after)

עַם   יַשְׁחִית   וְהַקֹּדֶשׁ   וְהָעִיר
(the people of) (he shall cause to be spoiled/mutilated/destroyed) (and the holy) (and the city)

נָגִיד   הַבָּא   וְקִצּוֹ   בַשֶּׁטֶף   וְעַד
(and until) (with the flow/flood) (and his end) (the coming one/the next) (the leader/ruler)

קֵץ   מִלְחָמָה   נֶחֱרֶצֶת   שֹׁמֵמוֹת :
(desolations, deserts, wastelands.) (is being decreed) (a war) (an end of)

Ok, let's discuss this. "And after the sevens, sixty and two, he shall be cut off, Messiah..." Unlike English, Hebrew sentence structure often places the verb before the subject. We would say, "The boy runs." The Hebrew often says, "Runs the boy." This is the case in this sentence. First the prepositional phrase, "...after sixty two sevens (weeks)..."), then the verb, "he shall be cut off", then the subject of the sentence, "Messiah." So we would translate, "After sixty two weeks, Messiah shall be cut off."

Let's look at the verb more closely. The reason the verb is translated, "he shall be cut off" is because in Hebrew the verb of a sentence must match with the subject of the sentence in gender and number. This is done by adding prefixes, infixes and/or suffixes to the root of the verb and by changing the vowels used in the verb. These prefixes, infixes, suffixes and vowel changes also determine the tense of the verb, whether it be past (perfect), future (imperfect) or present, and the person of the verb, whether it be first person, second person or third person. There are also seven different "patterns" for Hebrew verbs that determine things like whether a verb is simple, reflexive, intensive, active, passive, causative or other such type. If all of this sounds complex, you are right, it is. But I'll spell it out for you for each verb to make it easy for you to understand.

The root of the verb יִכָּרֵת translated "he shall be cut off" is כרת which means, "to fell" as in cutting down a tree. The prefixes and vowels (often called markings) tell us this verb is singular masculine third person, which is where we get the "he," imperfect or future, which is where we get the "shall," and is of the Niphal pattern which means it is passive. In other words, the action is happening *to* the subject not being done *by* the subject. Therefore, Messiah, which is singular masculine, shall, in the future, not *do* the cutting off, but shall himself *be* cut off. So we see from this that a tremendous amount of information is gleaned from the verb forms. Messiah shall be cut off, but not for himself.

Then the next part says, "...and the city and the holy he shall cause to be destroyed the people of the leader the next..." In English this sounds confusing but that's because Hebrew turns around the sentence structure once again. The subject of this sentence segment is "the people" and the verb is "he shall cause to be destroyed." As in the phrase before, the verb once again precedes the subject. And to make it more interesting, the objects of the sentence, the city and the holy, precede the verb.

The root of the verb יַשְׁחִית translated as "he shall cause to be destroyed" is שחת which means, "to be spoiled, to be mutilated or to be destroyed." The markings tell us it is masculine, singular, third person and future. Thus, "he shall." The Hebrew pattern for this one is called Hiphil which means it is causative. The causative form means the subject itself is not being spoiled or destroyed, but rather the subject is causing something else to be spoiled or destroyed. In this case, that would be the city and the holy.

But the subject of the sentence is, "the people." Isn't that *plural*? Shouldn't the verb form be third person plural? Ahhh. In English the word "people" *is* plural and thus we would use the term "they" to refer to them. But in Hebrew the word for people, עַם, is *masculine singular*. Thus the Hebrew would use masculine singular markings in the verb to refer to the people as "*he*" rather than "they." This will be very important to remember when we get to verse 27 as it will make clear some

51

confusions about the use of the word "he" in Daniel 9:27 of the King James Bible.

Now, just for complete understanding of the rest of this verse, let's talk about how I get the phrase, "...the people of the leader the next..." The King James Bible translates this as "...the people of the prince that shall come..." I suppose that's a reasonable translation but there is an assumption contained in this translation that is prone to abuse. Let me break it down.

First let me explain the mistranslation of the phrase, "that shall come." This "phrase" (הַבָּא) is actually not a phrase at all, nor a verb, but simply a single word used as an adjective. It more commonly is understood to mean, "next" or "the next one." There is no specific "future" tense to this word from which to get the word "shall." It is a combination of the definite article "the" (הַ) and the present tense form of the verb "coming" (בָּא). But what it really means is, "the next." Literally it translates "the coming" but the concept of the meaning is more like "the thing that is coming next" or "the next thing." It could be simply translated, "next." The idea of a future event is not explicit, but is implied by this because usually the "next" thing to come is future.

עַם is the word for "people" (masculine, singular). It is a noun. נָגִיד is also a noun meaning a leader or governor. King James calls him a "prince." This word is also singular and masculine. So, at first glance, it looks like this should literally translate as, "...he shall cause to be destroyed a people a leader the next." But there is in Hebrew what's called the "construct form" for nouns. It goes like this: When ever you have two nouns together in a sentence, the first noun is said to be in the construct form. This means the first noun "belongs to" the second noun. If I say in Hebrew, "servant king," this is translated, "a servant *of* a king." If I say in Hebrew, "servant the king," this is translated, "*the* servant *of* the king." Therefore, when I see in Hebrew, "people leader" this is translated as "*a* people *of* a leader. So this phrase could literally be translated, "a people of a prince the next." But "the next" is ambiguous. Even in the Hebrew, you don't know for sure if "the next" refers to the people or to the prince. It doesn't much matter, however, because the people are of the prince and they basically represent the same thing. The idea that there is another group of people and another prince coming is understood by referring to them as "the next" people and prince. This may have prophetic significance, referring to the people of antichrist and the man antichrist in the last days, or it may not. There is no way to tell for sure. It may just be a reference to the coming of Titus, whose people destroyed the city and the sanctuary. After all, we don't actually get to the 70th week until verse 27. It is entirely speculation to say from this text that the "prince that shall come" is a reference to the man antichrist. The word "shall" or even "the next" suggests a future event and fits nicely with the idea of the coming of the man antichrist in the last days. But I believe the text makes no such assertion. It is entirely speculation. Nevertheless, scholars from all over the world make this claim as being without question and teach from this verse that it is an established fact that the man antichrist in the last days will be a Roman. I'll talk more about this in a bit.

All that aside, the main point to keep in mind from this is that the subject of the sentence is "a people" and the word for "people" is singular masculine.

Ok, moving on. The literal translation of the rest of verse 26 would be, "and his end is with the flowing and until an end of a war, desolations are decreed. וְקִצּוֹ means literally, "and his end." The word "end," קֵץ, has the prefix "and," which is ...וְ, and the pronominal suffix, ...וֹ, which means "his." This pronominal suffix is third person masculine singular which could refer back to the subject of the phrase just preceding it, which would be, "the people," or it could refer back to "the city and the holy" which is itself also masculine singular. Most likely, "his end" refers to "the city and the holy" since this is what is being destroyed. If it refers back to "the people" then this part of the sentence doesn't seem to make sense since the people are not being destroyed but are doing the destroying. The word בַשֶּׁטֶף, translated, "with a flood," comes from the prefix, "with the," ...בַ, and the word שֶׁטֶף, which can mean flow, flux, fluency, torrent, gush, flood, inflow or outflow. So it's not necessarily a reference to a literal flood of water. I noted in the King James the next part is translated as, "...unto the end of the war..." This is not accurate because there is no definite article, "the," preceding either "end" or "war." Thus it should be translated, "...and unto (until) *an* end of *a* war..." Again, "end" and "war" are two nouns in succession and thus "end" is in the construct form and means, "an end *of.*" Finally, the word translated "desolations," שֹׁמֵמוֹת, is a plural noun that carries the idea of a barren wilderness or wasteland, a desert or backwoods. The idea is, I believe, that this war will desolate the land and turn it into desert wastelands.

So, let me summarize verse 26. After 62 weeks of years (following the initial 7 weeks) Messiah will be "cut off" but not for himself, and "a people" of a leader shall destroy the city (Jerusalem from verse 25) and the holy (which is most likely the holy sanctuary) and the end of the city and the holy will be by an overflowing (of an army?). And until an end to a war, it is declared that there will be desolations or waste lands.

Ok, now let's look at Daniel 9:27 and learn how it actually does flow nicely from verse 26. I put the whole verse up here but we are only going to focus on the first half:

9:27:

וְהִגְבִּיר בְּרִית לָרַבִּים שָׁבוּעַ אֶחָד וַחֲצִי הַשָּׁבוּעַ יַשְׁבִּית זֶבַח וּמִנְחָה וְעַל כְּנַף שִׁקּוּצִים מְשֹׁמֵם וְעַד־כָּלָה וְנֶחֱרָצָה תִּתַּךְ עַל־שֹׁמֵם

Let's break it down:

וְהִגְבִּיר בְּרִית לָרַבִּים שָׁבוּעַ אֶחָד
(one) (week) (to the many) (covenant) (And he strengthened)

וַחֲצִי הַשָּׁבוּעַ יַשְׁבִּית זֶבַח וּמִנְחָה
(and offerings) (sacrifice) (he shall cause to stop) (the week) (and the half)

וְעַל כְּנַף שִׁקּוּצִים מְשֹׁמֵם וְעַד־כָּלָה
(and until the end) (desolation) (an abomination or idol) (a wing or shelter of) (and on)

וְנֶחֱרָצָה תִּתַּךְ עַל־שֹׁמֵם
(on the desolate) (shall be poured out) (and is decreed)

Ok, I'm not so concerned about the last two lines, but let's take apart the first two. וְהִגְבִּיר is the first word of the sentence and it is the verb. This verb is singular masculine third person and is of the perfect or past tense. It is of the Hebrew pattern Hiphil which means it is causative. Causative

54

means the action is being done by the subject to something else rather than the action happening to the subject. The root of the verb is גבר which means "to be strong." The causative form would mean, "to cause to be strong" or "to strengthen." The conjunction "and" (וְ...) is prefixed to the word and the tense is perfect or past tense. The King James Bible translates this verb as if it was imperfect or future tense, but this is not correct. It is past tense and should be translated as, "and he strengthened."

The next thing to notice is that there is no subject in this sentence. This is permissible in Hebrew because the subject is implied in the verb form and refers back to the subject of the sentence before it. This is not an uncommon practice in Hebrew. The verb tells us we are dealing with a "he" and thus, it is not necessary to include the word "he" or any other subject in the sentence. Since the subject is missing, this form of the verb makes it clear we are referring back to the subject of the previous sentence, which was "the people." The masculine singular third person form of the verb matches the masculine singular form of the subject "the people."

What did he (the people) strengthen? He (they) strengthened "covenant." The word בְּרִית simply means, "covenant." I'll talk more about this below. The covenant is strengthened "to the many." The text doesn't tell us what the "many" is made of but the context would suggest the possibility of peoples or nations. The strengthening of the covenant is done for "one week." In Hebrew, when there are two or three of something, they say, "two dogs" or "three dogs." But when there is only one of something, they say, "dog one." Thus, "week one" means "one week." Then at "the half the week," or in the middle of the week, "...he shall cause to stop..." The verb is יַשְׁבִּית and the root of the verb is שבת, which means to stop, cease or rest. Once again, it is singular masculine third person, thus, the "he." And it is future, thus, the "shall." Also, once again, it is of the Hiphil pattern and thus causative. So the "he" does not stop. Rather, he causes something else to stop. In this case, what is being stopped is the sacrifice and oblation, or offerings.

So, in summary for verse 27, it is "the people" that caused to be strong "covenant" and they (he) did this "to the many" for one week or seven years. In the middle of the week, the people shall cause the sacrifices and the oblations to stop.

Ok, so now let's pull back and look at the larger picture. There are many implications to the Hebrew grammar that conflict with the more popular interpretations of this verse while at the same time the true translation reinforces (as we would expect) what we've already come to understand. Let me explain.

First, who are "the people" referred to in verse 26? Well, these would be the ones that destroyed the city and the sanctuary, which was done by the Romans in 70 AD. Since it was the Romans that destroyed the city and the sanctuary, and these are the people of this prince, the idea follows that the "prince that shall come," which some believe is a reference to the man antichrist, must also be a Roman. And thus, some reach the conclusion that the last day's kingdom of man must be a revived Roman empire. This whole idea comes from these few words in Daniel 9:26 but is nothing more than speculation. And the idea is not supported by a proper reading of the original text, as discussed above. Nevertheless, the idea has become so commonly accepted that it is no longer presented as speculation but rather as truth. Let me give you another perspective.

As I looked at all of the kingdoms of men that we studied in earlier chapters, I saw a consistent theme of antichrist. All of these kingdoms, including the Roman kingdom are kingdoms of antichrist. The people who are part of these political systems are also of the spirit of antichrist. Though I know it was literally the Romans that destroyed the temple and the city in 70 AD, the passage here does not specifically identify them as Romans, but rather simply as people of the prince the next. If, "the prince the next," *is* a reference to the man antichrist, then he is future. And the people of his political system are simply the people of antichrist. Now *they may be* Roman, but they may not. If they are not Roman and the next prince is not Roman, then those who have decided that they and he *must* be Roman will not recognize him when he comes. And when some other governing body that is not recognizable as a revived Roman Empire starts doing the things prophesied in the Bible, the "time of visitation" may not be recognized.

We already know without a doubt from chapters 7 and 8 of Daniel that there is going to be a man antichrist (the little horn), of whom Antiochus Epiphanies is a type and shadow, that will not be coming onto the scene until about three and a half years before the return of Christ. If we were to assume (contrary to the Hebrew text) that the "he" in verse 27 is a reference to the "next prince" and that this prince is indeed the man antichrist as claimed by the majority of prophecy teachers in the church today, this would conflict with what we discovered earlier. Such a belief claims that the man antichrist comes on the scene seven years before the return of Christ to strengthen the covenant. This does not agree with earlier prophecies that say the man antichrist comes just three and a half years before the return of Christ. But we've already seen how the Hebrew text actually speaks of the "people" and not the "man," and thus, we have no conflict with the earlier prophecies.

Ok, let's take this apart further. I believe it is clear from the original Hebrew of verse 27 that it is the *people* of antichrist that shall strengthen the covenant. But what is "covenant." Most today accept the Dispensational claim that this represents a new seven year peace treaty that is going to be made by the man antichrist with Israel. But, ignoring the fact that the man antichrist isn't even going to be around for another three and a half years, there are still some problems here. As we saw earlier, the word translated "confirm" in the Hebrew more properly means to "strengthen." But in either case, confirm or strengthen, the action verb is something that is done to something that already exists. You can't strengthen a friendship unless you already have a friendship. To create a new friendship is not to strengthen it or confirm it. So whatever else this covenant is, it is not some new agreement but rather an agreement that already exists.

As you recall, I already pointed out the use of "the covenant" from 9:4, and that it represents the Old Testament covenant of Israel that God made with Moses and Abraham. I also found some indications as to what "covenant" stands for in later chapters of Daniel. In Daniel 11:22, at the end of the verse, you see the phrase, "…yea, also the prince of the covenant." In the original Hebrew it does not have the definite article, "the" but just says, "…the prince of covenant." In 11:28 and 11:30 is the term "holy covenant" and in 11:32 it again refers to "the covenant" with the original not having the definite article, making it just "…wickedly against covenant…" These clues show how the word "covenant" is consistently used in Daniel simply to refer to the Jewish Abrahamic and Levitical covenants.

The use of the word "covenant" in Daniel 9:27, therefore most certainly is a reference to Israel itself and its covenant. This would make sense not only from the consistent use of the word in verse 4 and Daniel chapter 11, but from the fact that to "strengthen covenant" the covenant must already exist. The covenant of Israel most certainly already exists, but a "new peace treaty" would not.

So if I may be so bold as to put this first part of verse 27 into contemporary language, I would paraphrase it as, "The people of antichrist will give Israel the right to exist, or the right to re-establish their sacrificial rites, by confirming or strengthening their Old Covenant law." Israel's "right to exist" is questioned by many if not most countries in the world today. So this would seem to be a very plausible understanding of the verse. But it may only mean that Israel will be given the freedom to build a temple and reestablish their old covenant rituals of sacrifice. It may not be an official recognition of Israel's sovereign right to be a country by the Islamic nations of the world. It may just be that they will agree to allow Israel to rebuild their temple and once again practice the covenant of Moses.

Ok, the part that says "with many" in the King James is more properly translated in English as "to the many." It's a subtle change and not too significant, but the use of the word "with" is, I believe, part of what has sparked so much speculation that this is some kind of treaty "with" Israel. Most likely the only reason they think this treaty is to be with Israel is because the whole prophecy is about the people of Daniel, "thy people" (v.24). Most interpreters completely miss what I believe to be the obvious fact that the word "covenant" is a direct reference to Israel and not a reference to a new treaty. But there will be a confirmation or strengthening of covenant, which suggests *some* sort of agreement, "to the many." This suggests to me the idea that this agreement (which very well could be some sort of treaty) will be made by the people of antichrist with *other* peoples (not with Israel), possibly nations, to give Israel the right to exist or at a minimum the right to rebuild the temple and reestablish their old covenant rituals. These are, of course, speculations on what "confirm covenant" may mean. But Israel's right to exist is an issue in the world today which lends credence to that idea, and before sacrifice and oblation can cease as prophesied they must first be restarted. So something has to happen to make that possible.

Moving on, the rest of that first sentence of verse 27 says, "…and at half the week he shall cause to stop the sacrifice and oblation." So this helps us with our timeline. The word for "midst" in the King James literally means "half" or "middle" in Hebrew so this would say the ceasing of the sacrifice and oblation, which is stopped by "the people" of antichrist, occurs right in the middle of the final week of years. So there is a seven year period divided into two periods of three and a half years or exactly 1,260 days. Let's see if we can fit that last week up against our other timelines. (See figure 3 below.)

As we look at these charts there are some relationships that can be drawn. At this point, the only thing we can say for sure is that the ceasing of the daily sacrifices from Daniel 9 coincides with the suggested prophecy of the same event in Chapter 8. But there are some things we have to be careful of here. The events of chapter 8 as shown in the chart below were historically accurate and a part of the vision given to Daniel to show him of historical events to come. The fact that Antiochus Epiphanies stopped the sacrifices is historically true, and the fact that it was 1150 days, or 3.2 years before the temple was cleansed is also true. But when the angel began to give Daniel what appeared to be future prophecies concerning the man antichrist, paralleling him to Antiochus, (8:17-26), he said nothing of the stopping of the daily sacrifice or the years to purifying of the temple. He only spoke of the character and appearance of the man antichrist. So we don't want to make too much of this information. But there are several things that begin to stand out as we study what we know of the timelines.

We know from chapters 2 and 7 that there is a kingdom of men that starts with 10 kings. At some time, another king comes to power by subduing three of those kings. This king will then persecute the saints and make war against them. Chapter 8 suggests by parallel prophecy that this antichrist (and his people, Antiochus didn't do it alone and neither will the man antichrist) will cause the sacrifice and oblation to cease, but it doesn't say when. Therefore, we don't know how soon after coming to power that this man stops the sacrifice. We know from chapter 9 that this also occurs in the middle of the last seven year period of Jewish history. But so far what we don't know is if the end of the seven year period of Jewish history coincides with the end of the last kingdom of men, and we also don't know if the beginning of the seven year period coincides with the beginning of the last kingdom of men. There are, however, some hints.

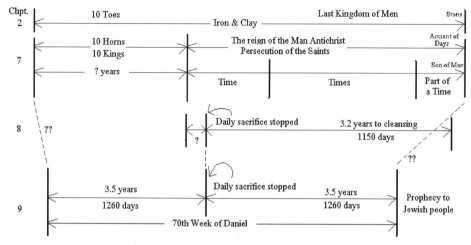

Figure 3: The 70th Week of Daniel 9

Verse 24 of chapter 9 says the end of the 70 weeks will "bring in everlasting righteousness." This could be a strong reference to the beginning of the reign of Christ which will also be everlasting and a reign of righteousness. Also, the "time, times and dividing of time" of chapter 7 might be a reference to "1 year, 2 years and half a year." If so, that would match the 3.5 years of the last week following the stopping of the sacrifices. And finally, in the second half of verse 27, it says, "[the people] shall make it desolate even until the consummation." That word "consummation" means "complete destruction" in Hebrew. That at least refers to the end of Jewish history, but could also easily be referring to the end of all things when the Stone returns to destroy the kingdoms of men. With these three hints, it appears very possible that the end of the seven year period could match up with the end of the last kingdom of men.

If this were true, then the moment the sacrifices are stopped must coincide with or be very close to the moment the antichrist comes to power and would tell us that the reign of terror and persecution of the church would last 1,260 days or 3.5 years. With me so far?

Now if the stopping of the sacrifice coincides closely with the coming to power of the antichrist, there are some things to consider concerning who "confirmed covenant." The confirming of covenant occurs at the beginning of the seven years, 3.5 years before the sacrifice and oblation ceases. It appears the man antichrist will not yet have come to power. This, then, would agree with the Hebrew grammar that says it was the

60

"people" of antichrist, or perhaps the 10 kings of the political system antichrist, who would be in power, that confirmed covenant. That may mean the reign of the ten kings is 3.5 years, or it may mean that they have already been in power for a time when this agreement is reached. After all, it only says the last week of years begins when covenant is strengthened. And if you say that it was the man antichrist that confirmed covenant, then you would have to say that he was in power when this was done, and his reign of terror would last the whole seven years. This makes the "time, times and dividing of time" meaningless, or at least not fit anything, and says the beginning of the last kingdom of men, ruled by ten kings, has to start well before the beginning of those seven years.

If you find all of that confusing, that's ok. I'm just reasoning and logically looking at what we know and what we don't know. Read through it a couple of times while looking at the diagram and it will make sense.

But putting that aside, here is what we know for sure. There will be a seven year period in the history of the Jewish people, and in the middle of the seven years the sacrifice and oblation shall cease. The Hebrew grammar states this will be done by "the people" of antichrist (most likely under the control of the "man" antichrist.) There was no seven year period after the death of Christ where "covenant was confirmed," in the middle of which the sacrifices ceased. They continued until the destruction of the Temple. The temple was destroyed in 70 AD after the crucifixion of Christ, and there has been no temple and no sacrifice since. In order for the sacrifice and oblation to cease, they must be happening. Thus, this seven year period must be a future time when the sacrifice and oblation is again happening. The Hebrew text of verse 27 says that "the people" of antichrist will strengthen or confirm the covenant of Israel for this seven year period of their history. It makes no reference to the "man" antichrist as the agent of this event. And in the middle of the seven years the people of antichrist (no doubt now under the man antichrist's leadership) shall cause the sacrifice and oblation to cease and the people of antichrist shall make the place desolate even until the consummation of their history.

5. The Greater Details of History and the Antichrist: Daniel Chapters 10, 11 and 12

Before studying this chapter, you should read chapters 10 through 12 of Daniel.

In these three chapters, Daniel once again receives a vision which, much like Daniel chapter 8, covers history from his present day through the reign of Antiochus IV Epiphanies. As an angel describes in chapter 11 what is coming he gives a great deal of detailed information about the events. Then in chapter 12 Daniel receives some more information concerning the timing of the events.

But first, let's look at chapter 10 verse 1. It states here that "a thing was revealed" to Daniel in the "third year of Cyrus king of Persia." That places the time of the vision to around 538 BC when Cyrus, the first king of Persia was in power. It says in 10:2 that Daniel was fasting three full weeks when, while next to the river Hiddekel, he had a vision of an angel. In verse 14 we learn that the reason the angel has come is to give Daniel understanding as to what shall befall his people *in the latter days*.

Two interesting things come from verse 14. The first is that the words of this vision are to help Daniel understand what is to befall *his* people. This would be the Jews. Thus, just as in chapter 9 and the seventy weeks, this vision is apparently from the perspective of the people of Israel and concerns things that are going to be happening in and around Israel. However, there are many terms and phrases used in chapters 11 and 12 that clearly associate the believers in Christ as being part of what's gong on. But as for geographical perspective, this vision is given from the perspective of Israel. This is born out in chapter 11 as the angel continually refers to the "king of the South" and the "king of the North." North and South of what? Israel, of course.

Also in verse 14 the angel speaks of what will befall Daniel's people, "in the latter days." This begs the question, "In the latter days of what?" In the vision the angel describes events which were future to Daniel but are now historical to us. The vision only follows history up to and including events surrounding Antiochus Epiphanies. Though he desecrates the temple and stops the sacrifice for just over three years, after that time the temple is again cleansed and the sacrifices and oblations continue. So nothing really "ends" in Jewish history here. There is nothing that one can point to in history at this time that would properly be referred to as the "latter days" of Jewish experience. Therefore, I believe the angel is giving us a clear message that the real purpose of this vision and prophecy is to give us information about what is to happen during the true "latter days," the last seven years if you will, of significant Jewish history. I believe the detailed descriptions of events that are now historically verifiable were given to demonstrate the accuracy of the prophecy, and to verify the validity of the events in the prophecy that are yet future to us.

Now when we jump to verse 1 of chapter 11 the angel says he also stood up in the first year of Darius the Mede to confirm and strengthen him. This may seem confusing at first until you discover that Darius the Mede ruled together with Cyrus from about 558 BC until about 538 BC, at which time the Medes and the Persians conquered Babylon.

In Chapter 11, the angel goes into amazing detail about historical events to follow. He speaks of the next kings of Persia, how Xerxes stirred up the Greeks and paved the way for the Greeks to hate the Persians, and how this prepared the way for Alexander the Great to come against them. Then he goes on and on about various wars and events that occurred between the "king of the North" and the "king of the South." These would be the lands of Syria and Egypt which were the two major divisions from the four that were divided after Alexander the Great.

I'm not going to go into this text and parallel it with the realities of history in this book. I could do so but it would take many pages. If you are interested in this, just go on line and search for "Daniel chapter 11" and with a little searching you should be able to find a site that will give you the detailed historical events of that time with the names of the kings and relevant dates and events that parallel those of Daniel 11. The accuracy of these prophecies is amazing and without error. So much so, that many down through the centuries were convinced that these prophecies were fakes, being written after the fact and not before. But why would we consider it an amazing thing that God could know the future since, as we learn in 10:21, these things are "noted in the scripture of truth." All of history is already written down in the books of heaven.

We will pick up our discussion with chapter 11, verse 31. But before I do, there are just a couple of things I would like to once again point out. In verse 22 we find the phrase, "the prince of the covenant." Historically we know that Antiochus IV killed the high priest of Israel, the prince of the covenant. But what I want to point out is the use of the term "covenant." This is the same word as used in Daniel 9:27 where it says, "…he shall confirm the covenant." It is not a reference to some agreement or treaty. The use of this word "covenant" in Daniel is always a reference to the covenant of Israel, the covenant of Abraham and of Moses. We find this again in 11:28, twice in 11:30 and again in 11:32. Because of these usages in Daniel 11, I am very uncomfortable with assuming in 9:27 that this is a reference to some new peace treaty, and not a direct reference to old Israel.

Now from 11:31 we begin to see events described that can only be referred to as *parallel* prophecies. I say this not just out of conjecture, but because, though many of these things did indeed occur historically with Antiochus Epiphanies, many of them did not. And in my next chapter on Matthew 24, we will find that Jesus referred back to these prophecies in Daniel, yet warned his disciples to watch for them as *future* events. Because of the words of Jesus and the many indications by the angel in Daniel 11 it is no stretch of the imagination to say that the events that occurred with Antiochus that are described in 11:31 through the end of chapter 12 can be considered as prophecies of events yet future to us.

I should also note here that there are some that would attempt to claim that all of the wars and battles described between the king of the North and the king of the South in chapter 11, verses 5 through 30, are also parallel passages and represent battles that will occur under the reign of the man antichrist of the future. Though I could not say this is impossible, I would say that this is a long stretch. Also there are no other prophetic Biblical texts to corroborate this speculation. For these reasons I would hold the idea lightly and spend little time trying to understand these described events in any way other than historical.

Verse 31: "They shall pollute the sanctuary of strength and shall take away the daily sacrifice, and place the abomination that makes desolate." If we look again at our chart below, this statement tells us where we are in the chronology of the last days; right in the middle of the seventieth week of Daniel 9. This places us at the beginning of the reign of the man antichrist and at the beginning of the (at least) three and a half years of his persecution of the saints.

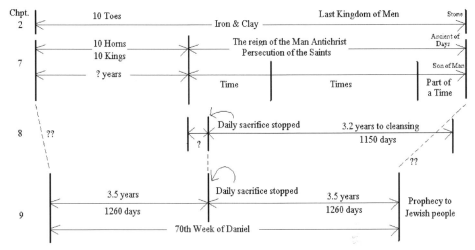

Figure 4: The Timeline So Far

Verse 32: Those who do wickedly against the covenant would be, in the time of Antiochus, the Jews that did not like the covenant of God (the Hellenistic Jews) but in our time would be those who do not like Christianity or the Jews. The man antichrist will corrupt them through flatteries. But the people who do know their God; in that time it was the Maccabeus that restored the temple, in our time it would be those who know Jesus; will be strong and do exploits. That's encouraging.

That suggests to me that during this time of persecution from the man antichrist, there will likely be a strong underground Church that will still be doing the works of Jesus and crushing the head of Satan. Though I know this prophecy was directed at Daniel's "people," and thus the Jews, I believe the Church will be tightly linked to these events because prophecy in both Daniel and Revelation makes it clear that the antichrist will persecute both the Jews and those that hold the testimony of Jesus Christ.

Verse 33: "They that understand among the people shall instruct many." This is a key verse for me personally. One of the reasons I did this study and wrote this book was because I believe there will be many in these latter days that will not know what is written in prophecy. Therefore, they will be confused about what is going on around them and frightened. My hope is to increase the number of people that "understand" so that they may "instruct many."

"Yet they shall fall by the sword, and by flame, by captivity, and by spoil, many days." Here is another description of the great persecution that is to come upon the Jews and the saints. This also helps place us on the timeline within the final three and a half years of history.

Verse 34: They will fall but will be helped with a little help. This is another encouraging verse that suggests there will be help for the Jews and the saints. It may be a reference to help from other people, but most likely this is a subtle hint of the help that will come from the Holy Spirit to do "exploits." "But many will cling to them with flatteries." This may be a reference to false brethren that cling to the church but are not really believers, or it may be a reference to those who would attempt to infiltrate the underground church in an attempt to expose them and eliminate them. I base this speculation on the words of Jesus, which we will examine later. But in either case, this is just more information about events within the persecution and something to keep in mind and watch for.

Verse 35: Here is a clear description of the purpose of persecution. Those of understanding, the wise of the church and the Jews, will be tried and tested. Some will fall. And this is to purge them and to make them white. "...even unto the time of the end." Again, a reference to the end. In the time of Antiochus there was nothing that could be pointed to that represented an "end" to anything. This must be a reference to the true time of the end, which is yet future.

In verses 36 through 39 we get some more information as to the personality and nature of the man antichrist. He will be a complete dictator that will, "do according to his will." He will be a horn speaking great and arrogant words against God, "he shall exalt himself and magnify himself above every god, and shall speak marvelous things against the God of gods." Then it says, "he shall prosper until the indignation be accomplished." This word "indignation" ties back to Daniel 8:19 where the indignation is tied to the "last end." The word itself means to "froth at the mouth in anger" which speaks loudly of the angry judgment of God that is to come at the end of all things. And once again, the use of this word more properly ties the prophecies of 11:36 with the future end of the kingdom of men, and not with the events of Antiochus Epiphanies.

The last phrase of verse 36 says, "that that is determined shall be done." Again, it is all written in the books of heaven. The future is not in doubt. God is in complete control.

Verse 37: "Neither shall he regard the God of his fathers, nor the desire of women, nor regard any god: for he shall magnify himself above all." Antiochus was an evil man. In Daniel 8:24 we learned that his power was not of his own. If not of God and not of his own, then it must be of Satan. These same characteristics will apply to the man antichrist. He will magnify himself to make himself god to all men. This thing about not regarding the desire of women may not be what it first appears. My first impression would be to say he has no real interest in women. Maybe he is gay or maybe he is just more interested in power and evil than in women. But I've also heard this phrase used in regard to Israeli women who hoped one day to be the mother of the expected Christ. This was called the "desire of women" in the old Jewish culture. This may be a reference to the fact that this antichrist cares nothing for this expected Christ.

The description of him goes on through verse 39. The last thing it says is he will, "...divide the land for gain." I'm not sure what this means. But given the current state of affairs around Israel today, I might speculate that when the man antichrist comes into Jerusalem and takes over the land of Israel he may divide up the land between the Palestinians and other Muslim factions that are right now vying for control of that land. Such a speculation suggests that the man antichrist may be of Muslim descent but that is not a given. I'll talk more on this speculation later in the book but for now that is all this is, a speculation in the Maybe Box. By the way, there is no historical record of Antiochus doing anything that could be described as, "dividing the land for gain."

In verse 40 we should note that it begins by saying, "...at the time of the end..." This is in context to the events that have been described in the previous verses. So it would appear the prophecy is saying that these battles that are described in verses 40 through 45 occur very near the end of the reign of the man antichrist, which, according to our chart, puts us at the end of the seven years of our 70th week and at the end of the last kingdom of men. So, apparently, there are several wars or battles that occur near the end, with the man antichrist making his last stand from

Jerusalem (vs. 45) or at the very least, from Israel. Shades of Armageddon.

As a last note on chapter 11, I want to point out verse 44 where it says, "...tidings out of the East and out of the North shall trouble him..." This should be noted and remembered for when we get into the book of Revelation there will be other descriptions of these wars that will reinforce and add to this prophecy.

Chapter 12 opens with the statement, "And at that time..." This can be confusing. Does it mean the events to be described *follow right after* the events that just ended in 11:45? Or does it mean *at the same time* as the events just being talked about in the previous verses of chapter 11? Is this a specific sequence or is it just a general reference to the time. It's hard to tell. The reason I bring this up is because of the phrase, "time of trouble." Some say the last seven year period is the "seven year tribulation" or the "great tribulation" period. Jesus, in Matthew 24:21, which we will get to in later chapters, specifically states the time of tribulation, which will be greater than ever was or ever will be, begins when the antichrist stands in the holy place and causes the abomination of desolation. So I believe that the time of great tribulation is the last 3.5 years during the reign of the man antichrist. But it is because 12:1 is ambiguous that some believe this verse suggests a "mid-tribulation" rapture. Those who hold to this would suggest the whole seven years is the tribulation and the last half is the great tribulation or "time of trouble." Thus, to them this verse would suggest that the "time of trouble" which would begin at the abomination of desolation would be the same time as the great deliverance of those written in the book, thus putting the rapture at the middle of the seven years. If this view is correct we should expect to find corroboration from other texts in the writings. In fact, there is none.

My view is that this verse kind of encapsulates all of the parallel events of chapter 11 that refer to end times, and thus all of the last three and a half years. This, then, is followed by a great deliverance of those written in the book. This would place the deliverance, or, as I'll discuss below, the rapture, at the end of the time period. Again, if this view is correct we should expect to find texts in the writings to corroborate it. In fact, there are many, and we will discover them as we go.

But setting that aside for now, if we just assume the narrative is following a chronological sequence, then Daniel 12:1 says that there will be a terrible time of trouble for Israel just at the end, such as has never been seen before, which just precedes the deliverance of the people, "…every one that shall be found written in the book."

Now, we know from multiple verses in Revelation and one in Philippians 4:3 that the book of life is the Lamb's book of life and only those who are to be saved are written in there. So this statement in 12:1 cannot solely be a reference to some national salvation of Israel. Those Jews whose names are in the book of life will be delivered right along with and at the same time as the Gentiles whose names are written in the book. So our deliverance must coincide with theirs.

Then verse 2 of chapter 12 adds, "…many of them that sleep in the dust of the earth shall awake, some to everlasting life, and some to shame and everlasting contempt." This is a clear reference to a resurrection. If this is a reference to a resurrection of the dead, then would it be safe to say the deliverance in verse one might be a reference to the rapture of the living? I think so. For verse 2 distinguishes the dead from the living of verse 1. So now we have some new information for our timeline.

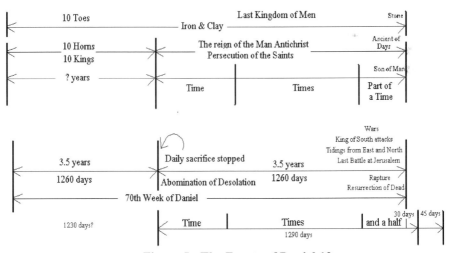

Figure 5: The Events of Daniel 12

Now we see toward the end of the reign of the man antichrist there are wars. "At the time of the end" he is attacked by the king of the South.

Other battles ensue. He will attack Egypt and take away their wealth. But "tidings from the East and the North" will trouble him and more wars will ensue. Finally, in verse 45 he sets up his last stand from the "glorious holy mountain," which I believe is Jerusalem, but none will help him and he will come to his end. At that time, 12:1, there is a great deliverance of all those found written in the book of life. The dead are referred to in verse 2 so verse 1 must be speaking of the living. This is very likely a reference to the rapture. Following that, or perhaps at the same time as that, there is a resurrection of the dead.

Finally, in 12:6 Daniel asks the question, "How long shall it be to the end of these wonders?" The first answer was simply, "…it shall be for a time, times and a half; and when he shall have accomplished to scatter the power of the holy people all these things shall be finished." It should be noted that this "time" is not the same Hebrew word as was used in Daniel 7:25. This word speaks of a set time and was commonly understood to mean a year. Also the word "half" here is the Hebrew word that literally means a half, which is different from Daniel 7:25 where it says the "time" was just "divided." Of course, this does coincide with the prophecy of 7:25 and the last 3.5 years of Daniel 9's 70th week.

I should point out here that this strange way of breaking down the last three and a half years is not likely to be without reason. If we understand the divisions to be one year, two years, and half a year, this marks two distinct points on the timeline. It will be interesting to discover as we continue through our study if there are any significant events that can be matched with these points.

The word "scatter" here means to break in pieces or beaten asunder. So this guy is going to really beat down on the saints during this period of 3.5 years and when he has finally shattered us to pieces all this will be finished.

Well, this answer wasn't good enough for Daniel because he didn't understand so he asked again what the end of these things should be. The first reply was to tell Daniel that the words are "closed up and sealed till the time of the end." Since the book Daniel wrote was not physically closed up or sealed, this must mean that the understanding of the book will not be clear until the time of the end. If this is true it behooves us all the more to be familiar with the words of this book so that when we see it coming about we will understand.

Next the angel says, "Many shall be purified and made white and tried.." which is another reference to the fierceness of the persecution, "…but the wicked shall do wickedly: and none of the wicked shall understand…" the unsaved and the unregenerate will have no clue what is going on, "…but the wise shall understand." The wise will have studied and come to know this book. They will understand what is happening and they will instruct many others in the truth.

Then the angel speaks the words of verse 11. A thousand two hundred and ninety days from the abomination that makes desolate. Well that's interesting. Half of a seven year period according to Jewish years would be 1260 days. This word says 1290 days. That's a 30 day difference. So now we have some questions. Does this suggest that the seven year period may actually be slightly longer, by 30 days, than an actual seven years? Or does it mean the middle, where the abomination of desolation takes place, is actually shifted left by 30 days so that the first half of the time is only 1230 days and the last half is 1290 days? I'm not sure. This much I do know; it will be 1290 days from the abomination that makes desolate until the "end of these things."

But then the angel throws a ringer into the story in verse 12 and says, "Blessed is he that waits and comes to the thousand three hundred and five and thirty days." That's another 45 days beyond the 1290. I wonder what that is about. I have sometimes speculated in the Maybe Box that this may be a reference to the time, after the return of Christ, that it takes to complete the campaign of wiping out all the evil of mankind over the whole earth, and then executing the judgment where the King separates the sheep from the goats (Matt. 25:32-33). That would take some time. And it would make sense that those who "wait" or as defined in Strong's Concordance, "adhere to" or make it to the end of the 45 days might be those who, though they were not taken in the rapture, survived the judgment and were allowed to continue into the millennial period. For we have already seen verses in Daniel that say there will be mortals during the reign of Christ the King on the earth. We have no way of knowing if this speculation is correct or even close. There are no other scriptures that shed light on or explain this 45 day period. Nor is there any explanation for the 1290 days versus the 1260 days. But they are there, so just be aware of them.

6. The sign of His coming: Matthew 24 and 25

You should read Matthew 24 and Matthew 25:1-13 and 31-46 before studying this chapter.

With the timeline structure of Daniel firmly in place it now becomes much easier to see how the prophecies of the gospels and Revelation tie right in. Without any stretching or reaching to make prophecy fit, but rather by taking what the prophecy says and believing it for what it is, we have found that the picture is not confusing or difficult, but instead there is a very clear timeline for end time events. Now as we get into the gospels and the words of Jesus we begin to get an even more detailed picture of what is going to happen.

Verses 1 and 2: The disciples were impressed with the temple and expressed this to Jesus. Jesus prophesied to them that there would "not be left here one stone upon another that shall not be thrown down." What he was speaking of was the complete destruction of the temple which took place just thirty seven years later in 70 AD. That's when Titus, the Roman general, came in and sacked the city and burned the temple. The war was so terrible that they ran out of trees to make crosses upon which the Romans could crucify the Jews.

The Romans never entered the temple or desecrated the holy place, which could have been interpreted as a fulfillment of Jesus' prophecy of Daniel's prophecy of the abomination of Desolation (which we will get to in verse 15.) Rather, tradition has it that when the Jews were pushed back to the wall of the temple area in a last stand against the Romans, a Roman soldier by chance threw a torch through a window and set the temple on fire. The temple burned from the inside with heat so great that it melted all of the gold on top of and around the inside of the temple and the holy place. The gold ran down around the walls and into the crevices of the stones. When the war was ended, the Romans dismantled the temple stone by stone all the way to the ground and scraped the ground clean. They did this not only to retrieve all of the melted gold but were also attempting to completely wipe all traces of Judaism from the surface of the earth. This happened in 70 AD. There has never been a Jewish temple since that date. In fact, there has never been a Jewish nation since that date, until, that is,

1948 when the Jews were once again given the land of Israel as their home land.

Therefore, since 70 AD, there has never been a temple, never been sacrifices or oblation, and never been a place where the "abomination of desolation" spoken of by Daniel the prophet could have taken place. Thus, all of the prophecies of Daniel and now we'll see of Jesus in Matthew 24 must be future to us. These are things that will happen in the latter days.

Verse 3: The disciples asked Jesus, "Tell us when shall these things be? And what shall be the sign of thy coming, and of the end of the world?" This is the question. We must keep this question in mind because this is what Jesus is answering. Many of the things in Jesus' answer could easily be applied to events throughout the history of the Church and even up to today. That's fine, but we must keep in mind that he is speaking of the time when "these things be," "the sign of [his] coming" and "the end of the world." Since we already know the basic timeline structure of the end of the world from Daniel, we know that the answer of Jesus will fit somewhere within this structure. Otherwise, prophecy would be inconsistent.

Verse 4: The first thing Jesus says is, "Take heed that no man deceive you." This is going to be a time of great deception. A time when we must be on our guard. Apparently, it is going to be much more difficult during this time to discern what is of God and what is not. The enemy will have learned many deceptive techniques and he will be going all out to deceive the elect of God. And this is going to be happening *in the Church!* That's why he was warning his disciples.

Verse 5: "For many shall come *in my name*, saying I am *Christ* and shall deceive many." They will come in the name of Jesus. They will say they are of Jesus. In fact they will say they are *Christ*. Well, they can't fool me. I know Jesus is not coming again as a man so all those guys out there claiming to be Jesus are just fools. And the people that follow them are fools. I won't be fooled by that, right? Or will I?

The word "Christ" actually means "anointed." Jesus the Christ means "Jesus the Anointed One." There have been a few nuts out there claiming to be Jesus. We are not fooled by them. But there are also multitudes of people out there claiming to be *anointed.* How many of us have been fooled by *them?* I know I was for many years. Many are coming in the name of Jesus even now claiming to be "anointed." But are they? One thing we know for sure from this verse: just because someone comes in the name of Jesus and claims to be anointed by God...*it means nothing!!* It means nothing. Take heed. Do not be deceived. In the latter days you will need to develop other ways to discern if a person is of God or not.

Verses 6-8: Wars and rumors of wars, but the end is not yet. Nation shall rise against nation (ethnic peoples against ethnic peoples) and kingdom against kingdom (country against country), and there shall be famines (starvation) and pestilences (epidemics of disease) and earthquakes in diverse (different) places. "All these are the *beginnings* of sorrows."

Ok, the beginnings of sorrows. Clearly these verses do not give us a definitive time on which to place them in our timeline. But if we are talking of the end times and the last kingdom of men it is reasonable to place them near "the beginning" of that kingdom. This would put them either just before the time of the ten kings, or during that time. For our timeline, since I believe Jesus is answering the disciple's question, I am going to place these events during the three and a half years (or more) of the last ten kings that reign early on in the kingdom. That would be prior to the coming to power of the man antichrist or the abomination of desolation. It would not be beyond the realm of possibility that these events continue on into the second half of the seven years or even occur in the second half. However, since Jesus referred to them as the *beginning* of sorrows, I feel comfortable for now placing them...at the beginning. (See figure 6 below).

Verses 9 and 10: Now begins the persecution. "They will deliver you up to be afflicted, and shall kill you: and ye shall be hated of all nations for my name's sake. And then shall many be offended, and shall betray one another, and shall hate one another." Because of the structure supplied by Daniel, we now see how we are moving into the second half of the seven years following the coming to power of the man antichrist. Here is where the persecution really gets going in earnest. Without Daniel, we would not know exactly where to place this. But because of Daniel we can be very confident in placing these events in the second half of the seven year period (Figure 6.) Perhaps we don't know precisely where in the second half to place them, but we can be reasonably assured they go in the second half.

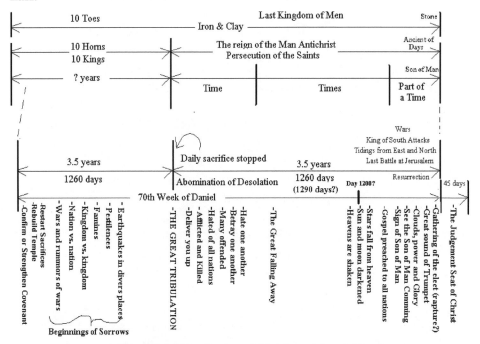

Figure 6: The Events of Matthew 24 and 25

Verse 11: "And many false prophets shall arise, and shall deceive many." Warning, warning! There will be false prophets! Do we know how to discern a false prophet? What if their prophecies seem to be right on? What if they are prophesying in the name of Jesus and showing signs and wonders (vs. 24)? How will you discern those who are of God and those who are not of God? Will you be able to recognize the imposters?

Verse 12: "And because iniquity shall abound, the love of many shall wax cold." What love is he talking about? I believe he is referring to the love of God. Because of iniquity and persecution, the love of God that the people profess to have will turn cold. Many will fall away from God during this time. This is why Jesus gives so many warnings. There will be a great falling away. Paul talks about this in 2 Thess. 2:3.

Verse 13: "But he that shall endure unto the end, the same shall be saved." This is a huge statement! The logical opposite of this is, "He that does not endure to the end, the same shall not be saved." It also makes clear that one can endure for a while and be fine, but unless that endurance

76

lasts to the end, he will not be fine. So much for the "once saved always saved" doctrine held by so many. But let's take this apart further.

What does he mean by endure? Well, though I might not know the particulars of how one endures, I think it is safe to say he is speaking of enduring in one's faith. In the previous verse he was saying the love of many would wax cold. It's the same thing. There has to be a strong foundation to your faith. It's not so much *what* you believe as it is *why* you believe it. What you believe is important, but it is the "why you believe it" that will determine if you endure. When the persecution comes and your life is on the line for what you believe, the question you will be asking yourself is, "Why do I believe that?" If the foundation of your faith is weak, it will not endure through persecution and trials to the end.

To the end of what? Well, reason would say either to the end of the period when Christ comes back, or to the end of one's life. Either to death or to deliverance, referring to the rapture. The point is, those whose faith endures to the end of their days, those are the ones that go in and are saved. If your faith does not endure, you will not enter in. If it were not possible to abandon your saving faith, then this statement would not make sense and Jesus would never have uttered it. This is a stern warning. The days are coming in which the saints will be tested to the hilt. If your foundation is grounded on nothing more then religion or ceremony, you will not stand. Your relationship with Jesus must be real and strong. Your knowledge of the writings, tricks of the devil and things yet to come must be sure. If your faith is not grounded in a true understanding of these things, you are at risk.

Verse 14: The gospel shall be preached in all the world, and then shall the end come. It does not say the Church must preach the gospel to all the world *in order for* the end to come. It only says that before the end comes, the gospel will be preached in all the world. Jesus is not trying to suggest that the end is dependant on this happening. He only says these two things will happen in this order.

The reason I make this point is because this verse seems to be the basic driving force behind many world missions organizations. Now I'm in no way diminishing the great work of these organizations, nor would I wish to see their motivation for salvation and evangelism diminished. But if they believe this verse places a mandate upon the Church which must be fulfilled before Christ can return, this is a misunderstanding and misapplication of this text. This text seems to be saying that this is a short event that occurs just prior to the end. The Church will be under massive persecution during this time. It's very unlikely that there will be any openly active missionary activities that can take place. Nevertheless, this event will occur but not in the way one might think. When we get to Revelation chapter 14 and look at verse 6 we will find this event seems to be taken care of by an angel. Whether this is symbolic of something else or not, it does seem clear that this will be a single short lived event and not the result of centuries of missionary work by the Church.

While I'm on this topic, let me discuss for just a moment how the erroneous interpretation of Matthew 24:14 is just another example of how men want to somehow make the Church responsible to accomplish something in order for the Lord to return. There are various theologies out there, many coming under the umbrella title of Dominion Theology, that follow this pattern. Some are convinced that we must get enough people around the world engaged in 24 hour a day prayer to pave the way of Christ's return. Others believe the church will gradually gain political power in the world by receiving divine solutions to the world's problems. And as they gain political power and political position they will gradually take over until they actually rule the world. If you don't believe that this idea is wide spread and prevalent in the Church do a Google search on "Reclaiming the Seven Mountains." Get ready for a shock. These people believe this must take place before Christ can return. Some even go so far as to say that when the Church accomplishes this task of taking over the world, then this constitutes the actual return of Christ to the earth because the Church is the "body of Christ." And thus, there is no physical actual return of the man Jesus. But his return is corporately accomplished through his Church.

All of these ideas, of course, put man up as king in place of Jesus. As they seek to rule the world, either through prayer or by actual political control, they are reflecting the same spirit as those men throughout history that sought to rule the world through military means. It is the spirit of antichrist. Whenever you see in the heart of a man, the desire to rule, whether it is to rule the world or to rule the local church as a pastor/king, know that this is not of Christ, but is antichrist. There is only one King. His name is Jesus. Any man who tries to become king in His stead, no matter at what level, is not of the Spirit of Christ, but is antichrist.

If those last two statements shocked you or sounded a bit extreme, turn with me to Matthew 20:25-26. "But Jesus called them unto him, and said, Ye know that the princes of the Gentiles exercise dominion over them, and they that are great exercise authority upon them. *But it shall not be so among you...*" [Emphasis mine.] And here is a similar statement from Luke 22:25-26. "And he said unto them, The kings of the Gentiles exercise lordship over them; and they that exercise authority upon them are called benefactors. *But ye shall not be so...*" The same is repeated again in Mark 10:42-43. Yet we still setup Church organizations with hierarchies of authority and make kings out of pastors. I'm not saying every pastor operates like a king, but the structure which grants such privilege and authority to these men makes it very difficult for most to resist it. By Jesus' own words this is not of Christ, but is antichrist.

Verses 15-20: "When ye therefore shall see the abomination of desolation, spoken of by Daniel the prophet, stand in the holy place..." Wow! Cool. Here Jesus gives us proof positive that the prophecies of Daniel concerning Antiochus Epiphanies and the events surrounding his desecration of the temple are parallel prophecies with the man antichrist and the events that will surround his day. Jesus said they would see this thing, "stand in the holy place." But it didn't happen in the next thirty seven years before the temple was destroyed. And there has never been a "holy place" since. Therefore, this event is still future to us. Of course, we already knew that because of the things we learned from Daniel. But here is the definitive statement from the mouth of Jesus, that the man antichrist will desecrate the "holy place" somehow in the last days. According to the timeline we already have in place from Daniel, that puts this event right in the middle of the 70th week of Daniel 9:27.

There are a couple of other things that are implied by this statement. Since there is no temple or "holy place" in which the man antichrist can "stand" then it follows that someone will have to build one. Whether it will be a full blown temple of stone or whether it will be a temporary tabernacle of tents where the sacrifices are again happening, it doesn't say. The closest thing we have to saying it might be an actual building is 2 Thess. 2:4. But somehow there will once again be established a holy place for the old Jewish rites of worship to take place. And speaking of the sacrifices, in order for the "abomination of desolation" to take place, which stops the sacrifices as we learned in Daniel, the sacrifices must be once again happening.

All of this points to the idea that somewhere near the beginning of our seven year timeline, Israel must again establish a temple or a holy place and begin the rituals of sacrifice as commanded in the law of Moses. What better time for all of this to begin to happen than when the "covenant" has been "confirmed" or "strengthened" to the many? (Daniel 9:27) This marks the beginning of the last seven years of significant Jewish history according to Daniel. Therefore, it is not a stretch or unreasonable to presume that these things will begin to happen right at the beginning of the seven years of Daniel's 70th week. (Fig. 6)

"Whoso readeth let him understand." This line in verse 15 was inserted by the writer of the text. These words were not spoken by Jesus. I believe this was inserted because the mystery of the parallel prophecies of Daniel 8 and Daniel 11 concerning Antiochus and the man antichrist were not known or understood. What Jesus was saying here was amazing and mind boggling to those who understood the historical fulfillment of Daniel through Antiochus Epiphanies. The writer of the gospel apparently thought this was significant and mysterious enough to point out.

In verses 16 through 20 Jesus says they should flee the area of Judea. Based on our timeline so far, it sounds to me like when the man antichrist uproots three of those kings and then comes to Jerusalem and does the "abomination of desolation," the persecution of the Jews (and the saints) is going to start off with a bang. Jesus says to flee. Get away from this guy. Hide. Why?

Verse 21: For then shall be "great tribulation" like never before or never again. Here is the definitive definition of "The Great Tribulation." It begins right here with the abomination of desolation, right in the middle of our seven year period. Many have referred to the entire seven years as "the tribulation period." I'm not so sure. From what I see in the writings so far, only the last three and a half years are referred to as "tribulation." It's possible and reasonable given what we know so far in prophecy to assume the first half of the seven years may be years of relative peace. The "covenant" of Israel shall be strengthened and the temple or holy place will be built, etc. It does suggest there will be wars and earthquakes and famines and diseases in various places during this time, which are called the beginnings of sorrows. But these things are already happening now to some degree. They will likely get worse during that period. But the real tribulation comes with the persecution of the Jews and the saints; with the coming of the man antichrist. That's when the real, the "great," tribulation begins to happen. It will be particularly bad in Judea and in Jerusalem. Jesus says to "flee," get away from there. It appears there is going to be some sort of war or battle fought there at that time.

Verse 22: "And except those days should be shortened…." How can the days be shortened? This idea of "shortened days" occurs three times in the Old Testament. Psalms 89:45, Psalm 102:23 and Proverbs 10:27. In each case it is obvious that the writer is referring to a reduction of the *number* of days, or in Proverbs 10:27, the number of years. Clearly the individual days were not literally shortened or reduced in hours, even though taking the words literally would suggest that. So, one would logically assume that Jesus was also talking about the *number* of days being reduced. But…this doesn't fit. We already know the number of days is *fixed* from Daniel. The days are counted and given in Daniel 12 as 1,290 days. How can the number of days be reduced when they are already established? This doesn't make sense. Does Jesus literally mean that the actual individual days are shortened or reduced in hours as his words suggest? Is there anything to corroborate this idea? Well, in fact…yes, there is. The days *can* and *will* be literally shortened. Jump ahead for just a moment to Revelation 8:12. Here we find text that describes how the days will literally be shortened by eight hours or one third, to sixteen hour days so that the "day shone not for a third part of it and the night likewise."

Verse 22 says if those days were not shortened, "no flesh would be saved." I'm not sure what this implies. At the least it implies that things are going to be really bad and a lot of people are dying. I don't know if this is a reference to people in general dying or if it is a reference to the saints dying in the persecution. But he does say that it is "for the elect's sake" that the days are shortened. How would shorter days benefit the saints? Well, I can only speculate, but here are my thoughts on this in the Maybe Box.

In the verses that follow (vs. 29) Jesus speaks of many monumental astronomical events, not the least of which is the sun going dark. We will find other scriptures later in my book, that I won't go into here, which suggest the Sun is going to go nova. It has already been scientifically shown that large sun storms, called coronal mass ejections, can minutely affect the rate of rotation of the earth. If the sun goes nova, it could literally speed up the rotation of the earth as prophesied in Revelation 8:12. No doubt this will be accompanied by massive earthquakes, changes in weather, maybe even a flip flopping of the magnetic poles of the earth. At any rate, things are going to seem to be totally out of control. If there were a heavily orchestrated persecution of the elect saints going on prior to these events, I can easily understand how such massive astronomical events might distract the people of antichrist from their murderous onslaught of Jews and Christians. And thus, by "shortening the days" many of the "elect" could be spared a martyrs death.

You can imagine by now in the sequence of events, many who have some knowledge of the Bible will be expecting the soon return of Jesus to the earth. Rumors will be everywhere. So Jesus gives additional warnings.

Verses 23 to 25: "Then if any man shall say here is Christ…" don't believe it. "For there shall arise false Christs and false prophets and shall show great signs and wonders; insomuch that, if it were possible, they shall deceive the very elect." False Christs and false prophets! They will come in the name of Jesus saying they are anointed. They will prophesy in the name of Jesus. In fact, they will assuredly believe that they are Christians doing the will of Jesus. Look at Matthew 7:22, "Many will say to me in that day, Lord, Lord, have we not prophesied in thy name? And in thy name have cast out devils? And in thy name done many wonderful works? And then will I profess unto them, I never knew you; depart from me, ye that work iniquity." They will assuredly believe they are Christians doing the will of Jesus. They will do many mighty works, prophesy and cast out demons in the name of Jesus. But they *will not be* of Jesus. We are given this warning from Jesus to watch out for these deceivers who are themselves deceived. Deceived by what? By their own flesh. For it is from their own fleshly desires of ambition, power, prestige, position and fame in the Church, all in the name of Jesus of course, that they are driven. They will believe it is their "manifest destiny" to spread the gospel and rule the world. But this is not the way of Jesus.

"…shall show great signs and wonders…" In the Charismatic Churches of today, what is the one thing people are praying for and looking for most (other than Jesus himself?) I would say; signs and wonders. We want miracles. And why not? People are sick and have needs. We need miracles. But according to Jesus' warning in verse 24, what does it mean when you see signs and wonders in the latter days? *It means nothing!!!* The enemy can also do signs and wonders. Just because you see signs and wonders in these last days it is no indication that this is of Jesus. You can not trust them. I do believe that the true saints will do amazing miracles during these days. But be very careful of seeing these things as evidence of the power of God. It may not be.

How much of that is already going on today? We see ministries all over the world claiming healings and deliverances (casting out demons). They are all done in the name of Jesus. Are they of God or not? How do we discern? There has to be some other way to tell. You cannot judge them by the miracles or by the use of the name of Jesus.

Maybe the thing you will have to look for is...*humility.* The spirit of antichrist wants to rule. It wants to control. It is arrogant and forceful. It may have a false humility, all the while claiming the "office" of prophet or apostle. Claiming authority. It claims a "manifest destiny" to do the works of God, to spread the gospel, to take the land for Jesus. But the Spirit of Jesus in a man will make him humble, gentle and dependant on the "providential hand of God" to grant success in his endeavors to serve him. There is a difference. It's not always easy to see. But we must watch. Those who are deceived by the lusts of their flesh will not enter in at the last day. The deception will be subtle and great. So great that, *if it were possible* (thank God for those words), even the very elect would be deceived.

"Behold, I have told you before." Be forewarned. Watch for it! Don't be fooled.

Verses 26 to 28: So now people are going to be saying Jesus has come. They'll say he is in the desert or in the secret room. But Jesus says don't believe them; don't go with them because his coming will not be secret or hidden. When we think of lightning in our culture we think it means "fast." But that is not the intent of Jesus here. What he means is it will be "obvious to all." In other words, when the lightning flashes in the East it is visible to everyone everywhere in the West. Everyone sees it. It can't be missed. The same theme is repeated in verse 28, "For wheresoever the carcass is, there will the eagles be gathered together." This text confused me for many years. I thought the word should have been "vultures." In fact, many translations do use the word vulture here. But I looked it up in the Greek and the word means "eagles." My confusion, however, was because I didn't know that eagles would eat carrion. I thought they only ate freshly killed prey. Then one day some trapper threw a number of skinned raccoon carcasses out along the country road just North of where I live. It was disgusting but the Lord used it to teach me something I didn't know. Within days, there were several bald eagles out there eating on the carcasses. I was shocked, but it made sense of this verse.

Still, that didn't explain why Jesus said this or what it meant. It seemed out of place until a friend of mine told me this is just a figure of speech. It's like saying, "If the shoe fits, wear it," or, "He's made his bed and now he must sleep in it." Those sayings have nothing to do with shoes or feet or beds or sleeping. Likewise Jesus' figure of speech has nothing to do with carcasses or eagles. What he is saying is, "My coming will be *obvious!*" In other words, it is obvious where the carcass is because that's where all the eagles are gathered. And when he comes it will not be hidden or secret or quiet. It will be bright, visible to all and it will be obvious. So don't be fooled by those who say he is here or there.

This also speaks to the amount of confusion that will be among those looking for his coming. Those who know these words in the Bible will understand. Those who do not will be led astray into many deceptions.

Verse 29: "Immediately after the tribulation of those days…" He is giving hints of the chronology of events. Look again at figure 6 above. All of this tribulation will be going on but right after these things the sun is going to be darkened, the moon will be darkened and the stars shall fall from heaven and the powers of the heavens shall be shaken. Wow! Big things are going to be happening. Some people try to spiritualize these claims saying he is talking about powers and authorities in the world of men. But there is nothing in this text to indicate that Jesus was being anything but literal. And these literal events will be confirmed by other texts in Revelation and in the books of the prophets and the psalms. It appears these things are going to be happening very near the end of the tribulation period.

So now let me take a slight diversion here and let's look at some numbers and have some fun. Remember how Daniel 12:11 said that from the time the daily sacrifice is taken away until the "end of these things" (Dan. 12:8) would be 1,290 days. We also know from Daniel 9:27 that the sacrifice and oblation is to end "in the midst" of that last 70th week of years. According to the Jewish calendar a year is 360 days. So if it ends right in the middle of the seven years, three and a half years would be 1,260 days. That's a difference of 30 days. What gives? Well, here are what I believe to be your only choices:

1. The "midst" of the seven year period is not actually in the middle. It is offset by 30 days so that the first half is only 1,230 days and the last half is 1,290 days.

2. The last week of seven years is not actually a precise seven years of 360 days a year, but is in fact 30 days longer than that with the first half being 1,260 days and the last half being 1,290 days.

3. Or, both halves of the seven year period are made up of 1,260 literal 24 hour days, but somewhere toward the end of the last half of those days the rotation of the earth is increased by one third so that in reality, in the same time period that we would normally see 1,260 *dawns,* we actually see 1,290 dawns.

If you follow what I mean by the third possibility it goes like this. According to Jesus in Mathew 24:22 and Revelation 8:12, the days are going to be shortened by one third to 16 hour days. This will happen sometime near the end of the last 3.5 years. If this is what generates 1,290 days or "dawns" in the same time it would normally generate 1,260 dawns, then we can calculate back from the end of the period and determine when this would take place. Here's the formula:

$$A * 24 = (A+30) * 16$$

In other words, how many 24 hour days (A) would be equal to that (A) plus 30 more days if the days were only 16 hours long? When you use your algebra and solve for A you get 60 days. Therefore, if the sun is darkened and the moon is darkened and the stars fall from heaven and the earth's rotation is sped up by one third 60 days before the end of the last 3.5 years, then you will experience 1,290 dawns in the same time that you would have experienced 1,260 dawns if the rotation had not been sped up. Sixty days before the end, or two months, is at day 1,200. (See fig. 6) *All of this is speculation,* of course, and in fact contradicted by information that comes from the seven trumpets of Revelation 8 and 9. So, though it was fun to play with the numbers (*Hey! I thought it was a cool idea until I got to Revelatio*n), when we get to Revelation, and specifically the seven trumpets, we will learn that the astronomical events of the heavens must occur *at least* five months before the end and more likely six months before the end of all things. (I'll talk more about that when we get there.) So this speculation is not likely to be valid and we still don't know what the 1290 days versus the 1260 days is about.

Verse 30: Shortly after the powers of heaven are shaken, "then shall appear the sign of the Son of man in heaven…" There will be a sign in heaven. The powers of heaven will be shaken. It's possible the stars won't appear to be in the same place they were before because it could be that the poles have shifted and the crust of the earth may have rotated on its core and all orientation to the stars will be confused. That's just a guess. But somewhere in the heavens, in the stars, there is going to be a sign of the coming of Jesus. I don't know what this sign will be and writings do not tell us. But those who know this verse and understand the stars will be best equipped to recognize this sign early on.

I won't elaborate too much on this here, but there is an interesting old book called The Gospel in the Stars by Joseph Seiss that describes the real meaning of the constellations and the ancient names of the stars. A more recent book, God's Voice in the Stars, by Kenneth C. Fleming also does this. I believe astrology to be a cheesy attempt by Satan to obfuscate the real meaning and purpose of the constellations and the stars, the names of which were given by God and not man (Psalm 147:4) and they were placed there for "signs" and seasons (Gen. 1:14). In reality, they tell the whole story of Christ from Virgo (the virgin birth) to Leo the Lion (the Lion of Judah.) The constellation group that speaks of the return of Christ happens to be Taurus the Bull. There are three deacon constellations to each "sign" in the zodiac. For Taurus these would be Orion the great hunter, Eridanus the river of fire, and Auriga the shepherd who holds a goat and two lambs in his lap. Taurus speaks of his coming in power, Orion speaks of his brightness and his coming in glory, Eridanus speaks of his burning and his coming in judgment and Auriga speaks of him as the shepherd who comes to shepherd his people. It's a beautiful picture of the return of Christ. Whether or not this sign of his coming will be in this constellation group, I have no way of knowing. But this is where I would watch for it in the night sky.

Another place that it might show up is in the "dark rift" of the Milky Way. The dark rift is where the center of our galaxy lies, and is found just between the constellations of Sagittarius and Scorpio. It is interesting that this point in space is almost exactly on the opposite side of the earth from Taurus the Bull.

Or, the position of the sign in the sky may not be related to the stars at all. There is nothing in the writings that says specifically that it is.

Also, just for fun let me digress a bit on some other little interesting bits of information. Most of you reading this book will have heard of the date 12/21/2012. This is the famous date on the Mayan calendar that marks the end of their "long count" calendar and supposedly marks the end of the world. Other ancient cultures like the Hopi Indians believe it will either be a time of destruction or the beginning of a new age of bliss. You can do the research on this yourself to get more details of their legends. What is interesting about the Mayan belief is that it held that mankind would either enter into a new age of bliss and happiness or into an age of destruction and misery, depending on whether or not mankind will have "evolved" into the higher state of consciousness and love and cooperation, or continued on a destructive path of division and hatred. The Mayans believe on this date that a doorway into the underworld will be opened and devastation and destruction will ensue. Others believe this depends on us and how we have evolved. It goes right along with the other satanically inspired ideas that say man is evolving into a higher life form. It also fits right in with the communist, socialist, antichrist ideas that say we must all join together in unity under a single controlling ideology and destroy all dissenters if we are to save mankind and live in peace. And then, of course, there is the Muslim idea of the 12th Imam, also known as the Mahdi, who will come during a time of great turmoil and chaos in the world.

But what's interesting is we are definitely coming into a time when we must each individually make a choice either for Christ or for antichrist. The mistake is, what they think is bliss is actually antichrist while those who reject the ways of the world and the idea that we are evolving into a higher life form that makes man into a god, though they may suffer

87

persecution and even death, will shortly after enter into the true bliss of the Kingdom of God.

But going back to 12/21/12, there are some interesting astronomical facts worthy to be considered. The Mayan calendars are based on astronomical periods, the movements of the moon, the planets, the sun and the stars and they are amazingly accurate. The Mayans predicted that on 12/21/12 our solar system, with the sun as its focal point, would be perfectly aligned with the central plane of the galaxy. There is some debate as to whether or not this is actually true. Some say there will be a *conjunction* of our sun with the center of the galaxy but not a true *alignment* with the plane of the galaxy. The difference is an alignment is a literal lining up of the sun on the central plane of the galaxy from the perspective of the center of the galaxy. A conjunction is when there is the *visual appearance* of an alignment of the sun and the center of the galaxy from the perspective of the earth. To help you understand, visualize our galaxy as sort of like a large fat pinwheel lying horizontally. Right through the horizontal center of this disk is the central plane which forms an imaginary flat circular disk, sort of like a CD. Our solar system (the sun), which resides about two thirds out from the center of the disk toward the edge, is supposedly right now just above that central plane and moving down toward it. On 12/21/12 some believe our sun will be passing through that central plane. But others say our sun is actually a long way away from the plane and moving away from the literal plane of the galaxy not toward it. Nevertheless, from the perspective of earth, on 12/21/12 it appears that the sun will *conjunct* with the center of our galaxy.

Now there are a few more interesting facts. Also on that day the sun, planets and stars will line up with the earth in such a way that you could draw a nearly straight line from the center of our galaxy, through the sun, through the earth, through Jupiter and into the heart of Taurus the Bull. The center of the galaxy, the sun, the earth, Jupiter and the constellation Taurus the Bull will be in nearly straight *alignment.* I say nearly because though the line will be straight from the center of the galaxy to the sun and to the earth, it then bends slightly to one side to pass through Jupiter and on to Taurus the Bull. That line may or may not lie on the actual central plane of the galaxy, but these things will be in near alignment with each other. What that means is, on that date, with all of this stuff lining up and all the myths of the Mayans and Hopis and the signs of end times from prophecy in our head, Jupiter will be bright in the night sky in the heart of

Taurus the Bull, the sign in the stars that speaks of the second coming of Jesus.

Does any of this mean anything? I don't know. Is this the sign Jesus is speaking of? I really doubt it because Jesus says in verse 30 that when they see this sign all the tribes of the earth will mourn. It's probably going to be something much more dramatic then Jupiter being in a constellation that most people don't even know about. And, after all, Jupiter passes through this constellation on a regular basis. Will something major happen on that very day on the earth? I have no idea. To be truthful, I doubt it. Maybe it will just be another "Harold Camping" moment that encourages the scoffers to say, "Where is the promise of his coming." (2 Peter 3:4) But it's all very interesting and worth being aware of and pondering in your hearts.

(Author's updated note: When the previous paragraphs were written, this event was still a couple years away. Today, February of 2013, this day has come and gone with nothing whatsoever happening to make it noteworthy. Jupiter, of course, is still in Taurus the Bull, and will be for a few more months. But it appears there is little to be made of it.)

But at a minimum we know there *will* be a sign in the heavens and then "they shall see the Son of man coming in the clouds of heaven with power and great glory." Remember Daniel 7:13? One like he son of man comes in the clouds of heaven. There will be clouds of some sort. So we add all this to our timeline of Figure 6. So now, in our chronology, he is coming. But Jesus isn't done. Something else is yet to happen.

Verse 31: As Jesus is "coming" he will "send his angels with a great sound of a trumpet, and they shall gather together his elect from the four winds, from one end of heaven to the other." I have a hard time seeing this as anything other than the rapture. But whatever it is, here are the things to note about this event:

1. This happens at the end *as he is coming.* Not after he has come and not before the sign of his coming.
2. There is a great sound of a trumpet.
3. They are gathered from everywhere (the four winds) from one end of heaven to the other.

There are those, mostly of the Dispensational persuasion, that say this is not the rapture, but a final gathering of those that were saved during the tribulation with the real rapture having occurred at the beginning of the seven years. To that I would say, so far we have seen no scriptural evidence of a rapture or gathering of any kind that occurs at the beginning of the seven years, or for that matter any other time than this one mentioned by Jesus. If there was to be such an event at the beginning of the seven years, it seems strange that Jesus forgot to mention it as he described the things that were to take place in the last days. He also said nothing about any such gathering in the middle of the seven years as some also suggest. Daniel also failed to discover such an event at the beginning of the time but did mention in chapter 12 that after a time of trouble his people would be delivered, those whose names were written in the book. But more importantly, as we continue to look at verses in the gospels and the epistles, not to mention Revelation, we will discover the Bible is very clear as to when the rapture will occur. It is so clear that I am at a loss to understand why there is any controversy on the topic. And just to make it abundantly clear for you, I have pulled *all* of the verses related to the rapture together into a comprehensive discussion and added it as an addendum at the end of this book.

Verses 32 and 33: Here is an example of a parable that I believe is not intended to be prophetic. Many suggest the fig tree is symbolic of Israel and that this parable is suggesting that when Israel comes back into the land then the end is near. In prophecy the fig tree is indicative of Israel. But this is just a parable. All he is saying is, just like a fig tree that puts out leaves in the Spring tells you Summer is near, so also, when you see all these things that I've just told you coming to pass, then you will know my return is "at the door." I believe that's all it was meant to say.

Verse 34: "This generation shall not pass, till all these things be fulfilled." Here is another little verse that raises controversy. I wouldn't try to make too much of this. Clearly Jesus was not speaking of the generation that was then living. If he was, then he was totally unaware of the fact that it would be some two thousand years before these things happened. I don't buy that, so he had to be referring to the generation living at the time the events he previously described were to be taking place. Since I don't believe the writings make it clear just how long a generation really is, and since we don't really know when that generation actually started, I don't believe anyone can make anything but wild speculative guesses as to how to apply this word. And for that reason I will spend no more time on it.

Verse 36: "But of that day and hour knoweth no man, no not the angels of heaven, but my Father only." Note that he only said "day" or "hour." He did not say "month" or "year" or "week." Though I know they had no idea of the time when Jesus was speaking these things, yet it is clear from his description of events and the parable of the fig tree, that he fully expected them to have a very good idea as to when it would be "at the doors." Too many people are saying "No one knows the time" because of these words and are therefore implying it is a waste of time to study these prophecies or to try to narrow the time down. This is foolish. These words were put in the writings on purpose to educate us on what to expect precisely so we *would* know the time when it begins to come to pass. If we are unaware of these prophecies we will most assuredly miss our time of visitation. Knowing these words gives us patience and strength to endure over the long haul of the years of tribulation. I will have more to say about this phrase, "no man knows the day or the hour" when we get to Revelation chapter 12.

Verses 38 and 39: His coming will be like in the days of Noah. No one will believe that these things are coming to pass; mostly because they will be ignorant of the prophecies. Everyone will be going about their lives oblivious to the fact that Jesus is about to come and destroy them.

Verses 40 to 42: One is taken the other left. I think this is another reference to the rapture at the last day as he is coming. Those that are ready will be gathered in. Those that are not will be left. It will be sudden. No one will know he exact day or hour, but those that have understanding will be watching and waiting. They will have heeded the warning of verse 42 and will be ready.

Verses 43 to 51: I'm not going into this parable in detail. Just note that the message is the same which is; watch and be ready for you do not know the exact time of his coming. Also, verse 47 seems to indicate that we will be made "rulers" over all the master's goods if we are faithful. This could be a hint in agreement with statements in Daniel 7 and Revelation 5 concerning our ruling and reigning with Jesus during his millennial reign (Rev. 5:10, 20:6, 22:5). Again in verse 50 he says he will come in a day or hour when they are not aware, and to those who are not ready, there shall be, "weeping and gnashing of teeth."

Matthew 25:1-13: The parable of the ten virgins. This little story perfectly encapsulates what Jesus has been trying to say throughout chapter 24...watch...be ready...those who are ready go in...those who are not do not. Many have tried to make much more out of this parable. But I believe it means nothing more than this. I'll explain.

The purpose of a parable is to make a point or communicate a message. In understanding a parable one should be very careful not to try to make every symbol or object used in telling the story into prophecy. Sometimes the purpose of a parable is to give you a prophetic picture of what things are going to be like in the future. Sometimes not. This parable of the ten virgins does. It gives you a picture of what things will be like when Jesus comes. The end message has a prophetic point to it. But that doesn't mean that all of the symbols or objects used to tell the story are prophetic in nature, or that they coincide with symbols used by the Spirit in the prophetic writings of the Bible. We should be careful not to try to squeeze such meaning out of the parables.

I bring this up because in the parable of the ten virgins, many go to great lengths to attempt to equate the oil in the lamps with the Holy Spirit, just as the anointing oil of the Old Testament was prophetically symbolic of the Holy Spirit. But when you do this you must now try to make sense of the story and explain how the Holy Spirit can "run out" (vs. 25:8). I've heard some strange explanations. But if you separate yourself from this requirement and just read the story for the message Jesus is attempting to deliver, and he is doing so in the context of the message he was delivering in chapter 24, you will find that it is totally consistent and easily understandable. Let's go through it.

In verse 1, Jesus says, "Then shall the kingdom of heaven be like.." So he has placed this story in the timeline right near the end when the "bride groom comes." The kingdom of heaven won't be *exactly* like this, but it will be *similar* to this. It will be like, "...ten virgins which took their lamps and went forth to meet the bride groom." Ok, I don't really know that much about the wedding traditions of the Jews. My understanding is, when the couple is officially engaged to be married, the groom then goes off and builds a house for them. When he is done he comes back to get his

92

bride, and that's when the ceremony takes place, and then he takes his bride into his house and shuts the door. I could be way off on that but its something like that. Anyway, Jesus is using this picture of the typical ceremony surrounding a traditional Jewish wedding.

Regardless of all of that, in this story there are ten virgins who take their lamps (must be night?) and are waiting for the bride groom. It would seem obvious that these virgins represent the Church, for it will be the believers that are waiting for the return of their King and groom Jesus Christ.

Verse 2: All of the virgins are the same. The *only* difference is, five are wise and five are foolish. Many who believe in the "once saved always saved" doctrine believe the five foolish virgins were not really Christians. They have to say that because the five foolish virgins do not get into heaven in the end. Therefore, in order to fit the parable to their doctrine, they must project the five foolish virgins as "deceivers" who are actually lost. It makes no sense. You should not attempt to squeeze the meanings of the texts into your doctrines, but rather should form your doctrines from what is written. The reality is *there was no difference in the virgins* except that five were wise and five were foolish. They were all virgins, they were all waiting for the same bridegroom, they were all carrying lamps, all of the lamps were burning with oil and they all slumbered and slept. The only difference was that the foolish virgins did not have enough oil so that their lamps could, *"endure to the end."*

The foolish virgins believed that the time would be short. (Perhaps they thought the rapture would come early and save them from the tribulation?) But in reality, the coming of the bridegroom was delayed and the lamps of the foolish virgins did not endure unto the end.

Tying this to the context of chapter 24, it seems to me that the light of the lamps of the virgins represents their faith, and the oil that keeps that faith burning represents the *foundation* upon which their faith is based. Remember the persecution during this time? This parable doesn't directly speak to that part of the story. But we know this is going to be going on. The only thing that will keep your faith burning so that it will endure to the end will be the depth of the foundation of your faith; the stuff your faith is based on. That's the oil.

So now, in verse 6, the bridegroom comes and they all jump up to trim their lamps. But the lamps of the foolish have not endured. They go to the wise and ask for more oil. The wise tell them they cannot give of their oil or there will not be enough for them both, but they must go to those who sell and buy more. Now don't try to turn every event in the parable into a prophetic event on the timeline. It doesn't work. Just look for the message. And don't try to make too much of this, "lest there be not enough for us and you." The point is you cannot just give of your experience, your relationship and your knowledge of Christ to another in a moment. It takes time. The foolish virgins had to go to those who sell and buy for themselves. We must all build our own experience, knowledge of the writings, faith and relationship with the Lord. You must build your own foundation for your faith. This does not generally happen in a day. It takes time.

Now is the time. Now is the time to work with the "foolish" virgins to teach them and encourage them to build that foundation, to build up the reserve of oil, so that in the day of persecution their lights will endure to the end. Now is the time to let them know of the urgency, of the need to be no longer "foolish" or complacent. Now is the time to educate them in the writings so they will know the bridegroom is going to tarry. That it will be a long hard wait. That they will be tested to the hilt with deception and trials and persecutions. Now is the time!

Because, as in verse 10, while they were going the bridegroom came…and it was too late. Those that were ready, that endured, went in and the door was shut. (This is again perhaps another loose reference to the rapture.) But the door is shut. When the foolish return they cry to the Lord to open unto them, but he says, "I know you not." Sounds very much like Matthew 7:22 and 23.

So in verse 13, the message of the parable is given, "Watch therefore." Be ready. It will be a long haul. You don't know the day or hour of his return. Don't assume it will be short or easy. Get lots of oil. Go deep. Test your relationship. Test your faith. Know the writings of the Bible. Be ready. Be wise. Now is the time to be doing that, before it is too late.

The only other part of chapter 25 I want to cover is verses 31 to 46. This adds another event to our timeline. Jesus says, "When the Son of man shall come in his glory, and all the holy angels with him, then shall he sit upon the throne of his glory…" Thus he begins to describe what is commonly referred to as the "Judgment Seat of Christ." Jesus shall separate the sheep from the goats. There is no text here to determine if he is speaking of those who have died and been raised or raptured or those who are still alive and living on the earth after his return. I tend to believe this has to be those who are raised in the spirit because the end of this judgment is that the sheep go into heaven and the goats go into everlasting punishment. I don't believe this event involves those who survive alive on earth into the millennium.

It's a long parable and I only want to point out a couple things. I noted in verses 34 and 40 Jesus now refers to himself as the "King." Indeed he is. I also noted a distinct difference in the attitudes of the sheep and the goats. When the King tells the sheep what they have done and why they are entering into the Kingdom prepared for them, the sheep answer *in humility*, "when did we do these things?" But when the King tells the goats what they have done and why they are entering into everlasting punishment, their response is *in arrogance and pride*, "when did we *not* do these things?" I believe as we enter into these last days of elaborate and subtle deceptions in the Church it will only be the ability to discern these attitudes that will be the true indicator of who is of Christ and who is of antichrist. The time is upon us, for antichrist is already among us, and the deceptions are already ravaging the Church (1 John 2:18). Watch therefore, and discern.

7. The sign of His coming: Mark 13 and Luke 21

You should read Mark chapter 13 and Luke chapter 21 before beginning this study.

This chapter will be relatively short since Mark 13 is almost a repeat of Matthew 24. Luke 21, which is Luke's version of this same event, adds only a slightly different perspective.

In Mark 13:4 the story starts off just as in Matthew. The disciples ask Jesus when these end times things will be and what will be the sign when these things will be fulfilled. As in Matthew, the first thing Jesus says is, "Take heed lest any man deceive you." The warning is in all three accounts. Watch for the deceptions.

Mark continues with the "wars and rumors of wars," kingdoms against kingdoms, nations against nations and earthquakes in diverse places. Mark also calls these, "The beginnings of sorrows." Following that, just as in Matthew, he begins to talk of the persecutions of the saints and the Jews.

Verse 10: As in Matthew 24:14, Jesus mentions that, "This gospel must first be published among all nations." And according to Revelation14:6, it appears this is done through the agency of an angel, rather than a missions board. But when we get into Revelation, we will find that one way this could be fulfilled is through the *two witnesses*.

Starting in verse 12, Mark adds a bit more detail about the "betrayals" that Matthew talks about. Matthew just says in 24:10 that many will betray one another. Mark adds that, "brother shall betray the brother *to death*, and the father the son; and children shall rise up against their parents and *shall cause them to be put to death.*" It's going to be a very difficult time. As communism and socialism, and perhaps Islamic extremism, spreads throughout the world, and allegiance to the antichrist becomes mandatory, many who are deceived will betray their own blood kin to death in the illusionary quest for human unity.

Verse 13: As in Matthew, Mark repeats the statement "…he that endures unto the end, the same shall be saved." Which means: He that does not endure to the end shall not be saved.

Verse 14: Mark mentions the abomination of desolation just as Matthew, and also adds the same little parenthesis, "(let him that readeth understand.)" This almost suggests that one or the other copied much of their rendition of this event from the other. Nevertheless, Mark only says that the abomination of desolation "stand[s] where it ought not" while Matthew says, "stand[s] in the holy place." Regardless, the result is the same: the people should run away and hide. Clearly there is going to be war and a lot of mayhem in Jerusalem and/or Judea when this happens.

Verse 19: Mark calls it "affliction" instead of "great tribulation" as Matthew does. Nevertheless, it will be great affliction as was never before or after.

Verse 20: Again we hear the account where Jesus says, "…the Lord had shortened those days…" As before, because of Revelation 8:12, I believe this is a literal shortening of the 24 hour day to 16 hours. The ramifications of this for catastrophic changes on the surface of the earth are enormous. Note that Mark adds the words, "…whom he hath chosen…" to Jesus' statement. I don't know that this is a significant addition, but noted the difference.

Verse 22: As before, Jesus continues to warn of false Christs and false prophets showing signs and wonders "to seduce" even the elect. That's a slight difference from Matthew. Matthew says these signs and wonders, if possible, would "deceive" the very elect while Mark says they are purposely designed to "seduce" the very elect…if it were possible. There *is* an enemy…and he *is* out to get you.

Verse 24: After the tribulation the sun and moon are darkened and the stars fall and the powers that are in heaven shall be shaken. It's going to be catastrophic. This sounds a lot like all the movies that have been made about 2012. However, from these accounts, it appears to me that these events occur near the end of the seven years. December 21, 2012, is just over a year and a half away from the date of this writing (April, 2011). I believe that is too close. It does not appear that we have seen the signs of the beginning of the seven years, which would be a world wide government ruled by ten kings and some sort of agreement with Israel that strengthened or confirmed their Old Covenant. Therefore, I don't believe these astronomical events will occur on that date in 2012. But I believe they could certainly occur within a few short years after, assuming the start of the seven year period is near. Perhaps 12/21/12 will mark the start of the seven years. After all, that is just two months following the next presidential election in the US. It could be that the world governance groups that are trying to form a global governance will hold off until after the elections just to see if they still have a partner for this endeavor in the white house. Just a thought. But the way things are going in the world today, I'm beginning to think the beginning of the seven years could be as early as October of this year. More on this when I get to Revelation 12.

(Author's update note: Obviously, as of February 2013, the signs of the beginning of the last 7 years have not yet occurred. Mr. Obama *was* re-elected last year so I'm sure things are moving forward on the one world government at break neck speed. Since the signs were not seen in Oct. of 2011 nor that same time period in 2012, I am looking for the signs any year now. As I say above, I will have more detail on this when I get to Revelation chapter 12.)

Verse 26: Mark doesn't mention the "sign of the Son of man in the heavens" but rather goes right to the, "Son of man coming *in the clouds* with great power and glory." This is all very much the same as Matthew.

Verse 27: The gathering then occurs. Mark doesn't mention the trumpet as Matthew does, but does add that the gathering is not only from the far reaches of heaven but also, "from the uttermost parts of the earth." Again, this is a strong indication that Jesus is speaking of the rapture. And once again it is significant that Jesus made no mention of any other gathering of saints in any form or at any other time during his description of end time events. Thus, I believe to suggest that there is a gathering or rapture of the saints at any other time is wishful thinking at best and intellectual dishonesty at worst.

The rest of the chapter is very much like Matthew 24 so I won't belabor things here. At this point, our timeline remains basically unchanged from our last chapter and looks like this:

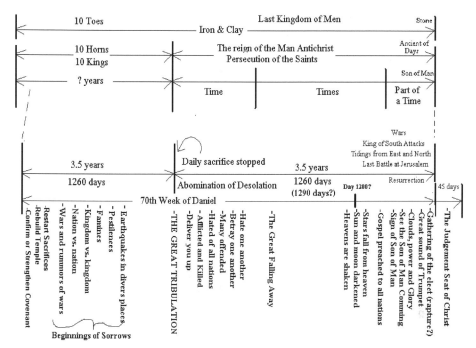

Figure 7: Timeline from Mark 13

Now we turn to Luke 21. In this section of the writings we see a slightly different perspective. Much of it is as it was in Matthew 24 and Mark 13. However, in verses 11 and 12, we see that Luke lists earthquakes, famines and pestilences right along with fearful sights and great signs from heaven. This sort of ties what Matthew and Mark called "the beginning of sorrows" with the astronomical events that occur closer to the end of the second half of the seven years. This would tend to place the "beginning of sorrows" in the second half of the timeline. Luke then appears to confirm this new order of things by starting verse 12 with "Before all these they shall lay hands on you…" So Luke is saying the persecution begins *before* these events that were referred to as "the beginning of sorrows."

I only placed the "beginning of sorrows" in the first half with Matthew and Mark because it seemed reasonable, given what it was called, to place them near the beginning. But now, from Luke, we get a clearer picture of where they should really go. In actuality, I believe we will find as we get into Revelation that this better order of events is confirmed. So now, look at figure 8 below and notice what appears to be a better order of events. This makes more sense as one would expect the earthquakes and wars and pestilences, etc, to more closely precede and lead up to the final astronomical cataclysmic events. Note in the figure that the many events that begin to occur near the end of the period take up much too much space on the timeline. The positions of the events are *not to scale.* It is likely that all of these events will occur bunched around or just preceding the beginning of the last six months. We'll discover why I say this with the trumpets in Revelation. So keep in mind that these events probably start somewhat later than they appear on the line as presented in Figure 8. But some of them, such as the wars and famine and disease, could begin earlier and continue to increase as the cataclysmic events approach.

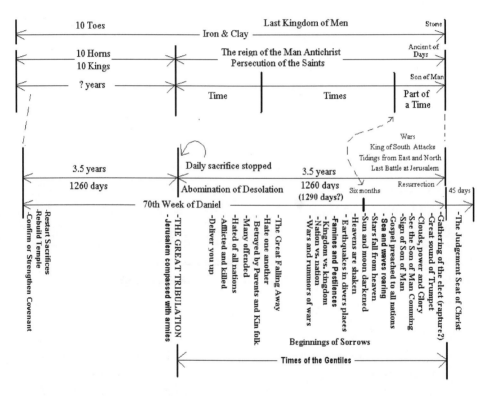

Figure 8: The Events of Luke 21

Verse 15: A wonderful promise of Jesus that when the persecutors bring us before kings and rulers the Lord will give us words to speak and a "mouth and wisdom which all your adversaries shall not be able to gainsay nor resist."

100

Verse 18: This statement isn't found in Matthew or Mark but is a very important promise to encourage the saints during this difficult time. "...not one hair on your head will perish." I like to joke that this is very encouraging for bald men because it says all of those hairs are up there in heaven waiting for us. But putting humor aside, this statement will one day become a rallying cry of encouragement for a people being betrayed daily to death. As a saint of God, you cannot die. If your body dies you simply go home and rest from your labors. They cannot win. They cannot destroy you. They can only send you home. Not one hair of your head shall perish.

Verse 19: "In your patience posses ye your souls." The victory is won in the waiting. Wait for the Lord. "Vengeance is mine, I will repay saith the Lord." (Romans 12:19) Hold fast to your faith, keep the lamp lit and trust in him. He will come.

Then in verse 20 we learn something new. Matthew and Mark both said, "When you shall see the abomination of desolation..." but Luke records that Jesus said "When ye shall see Jerusalem compassed with armies then know that the desolation is near." The words that follow instructing the people to flee are the same as recorded in Matthew and Mark. Thus we know that he was speaking of the same event. So it appears that just prior to the abomination of desolation, Jerusalem will be surrounded by armies. This confirms the thought that there is going to be some sort of battle or war at this time, and also gives us another sign to watch for to mark this point in history. We can also add this to our timeline. (Fig. 8)

Verses 23 and 24: I just want to point out that Jesus says here, "...great distress in the land, and wrath upon *this people*." Clearly there is going to be an attack on Jerusalem and the people of Israel. It will be bad. This is why Jesus says to flee and not look back. In verse 24 he says they shall fall by the sword and be led away captive into all nations. And then he says, "...and Jerusalem shall be trodden down of the gentiles until the times of the gentiles be fulfilled." Now there is no shortage of theories and claims about what and when the "times of the gentiles" is supposed to be. Many think it started with the captivity of Israel in Babylon and continues to this day. But regardless, all of these ideas are just opinions and assumptions based on nothing more than speculation. There are no verses in the writings to support any of these ideas, because, you see, this term, "the times of the gentiles," is not used or mentioned anywhere else in the Bible. All we know about it is what is right here in these verses. Thus, to take this term and attempt to turn it into an "age" or a spiritual measurement is a stretch in the extreme.

The answer to this is simple. Jesus was talking about when the antichrist would surround Jerusalem and then stand in the holy place "where he aught not" to commit the abomination of desolation. This is the Gentiles trodding Jerusalem under foot. And this will continue, according to our timeline, until the end of the three and a half years of the great tribulation. You might say I'm also guessing and stretching to add my own idea to the list. But if you look at Revelation 11:2 you find confirmation of my claim. Though the measuring of the temple is a prophetically symbolic action in the book, the Lord gives a distinctly non-symbolic explanation for why John should not measure the outer court, "…for it is given unto the Gentiles: and the holy city shall they tread under foot forty and two months." How long is forty two months? Three and one half years. As we get into these verses in Revelation in context we will see clearly that this is the same period of time as the great tribulation when the man antichrist is ruling the world and persecuting the saints.

Verses 25 and 26: We have here the usual signs in the sun and moon and stars but then he adds, "…upon the earth distress of nations with perplexity, the sea and the waves roaring." There will be much confusion and destruction and, not surprisingly with earthquakes, tsunamis from the sea. A great example of what this may be like would be the great quake and tsunami of Japan on March 11 of 2011. Men's hearts will be failing for all the terrible things that are coming upon the earth for the powers of heaven shall be shaken.

Verses 27 and 28: As in the other two gospels, then shall they see the Son of man coming in a *cloud* and with power and great glory. But Luke doesn't mention a gathering at this time. Instead, he just records Jesus as saying, "And when these things begin to come to pass, then look up, and lift up your heads; for your redemption draweth nigh." It sounds to me like he is saying the gathering is near. The rapture is at hand. Look up. Lift up your heads. The Kingdom comes.

Most of the rest of Luke 21 is similar to what we found in Matthew and Mark. But there is one more verse I need to expand upon. This is verse 36. Here Jesus is recorded as saying, "Watch ye therefore, and pray always, that ye may be accounted worthy to escape all these things that shall come to pass, and to stand before the Son of man." This verse is often used to encourage the idea that the church is raptured out before the time of the tribulation. It is said that those that are counted "worthy to escape" will do so by being taken up early. But, once again, this is a stretch in an attempt to justify an idea that came from man's imagination, and not from the writings. There are other ways one might escape the things to come. He may be hidden and protected in a secret place, or he may die, or he may be martyred. There is nothing to say this refers to a rapture. And with no other texts in the writings to directly support the idea of a rapture at any other time than the end of the tribulation, one would be justified in rejecting this interpretation of this verse. See the addendum at the end of this book for more on this subject.

8. The Seven Seals: Revelation Chapters 6 and 7

You should read Revelation, chapters 1 through 7 before studying this chapter.

Most people, when they think of end time prophecy, think of the book of Revelation. And that book is indeed filled with information about the last days. But without the foundational structure that has now been built by going through Daniel and the gospels, much of what we find in this book would be very difficult if not impossible to place on a timeline. There are not many hints in Revelation by itself just exactly when or in what order the things that are revealed here happen. But with the clear framework of Daniel, and the detailed accounts of Jesus in the gospels, it becomes much easier, and in fact in most cases obvious, to determine where in the timeline these events occur.

The real meat of events doesn't begin until chapter 6 and the seven seals. But before we start into these, if you haven't already done so, I strongly encourage you to read chapters 1 through 5. This sort of sets the stage for the vision that John is receiving and puts the events of the vision in context.

Also, before we do the seals, I'd like to record here some prophetic statements in Revelation that Jesus made at the end of each of those letters to the churches that he is reciting. Though they do not clearly fit on any timeline, they do add to the prophetic picture or "atmosphere." Here they are:

Chapter 2, verse 7: "He that hath an ear, let him hear what the Spirit saith unto the churches: To him that overcometh will I give to eat of the tree of life, which is in the midst of the paradise of God." Cool! The Tree of Life is coming back. The last time we heard of that tree was in the Garden of Eden. Apparently, God's not done with this tree as yet, and apparently, we will partake of its fruit.

Chapter 2, verses 10b-11: "Be thou faithful unto death and I will give thee a crown of life. He that hath an ear, let him hear what the Spirit saith unto the churches; He that overcometh shall not be hurt of the second death." The second death. The first death would be the separation of the soul from the body. The second death would be the separation of the soul from God. We will also learn in Revelation 20:14 that this is referred to as the Lake of Fire.

Chapter 2, verse 17: "He that hath an ear, let him hear what the Spirit saith unto the churches; To him that overcometh will I give to eat of the hidden manna, and will give him a white stone, and in the stone a new name written which no man knoweth saving he that receiveth it." I don't know what the hidden manna or the white stone with a new name on it is all about. But it sounds cool, and I'll be watching for this when the time comes.

Chapter 2, verses 25-28: "But that which ye have already hold fast till I come. And he that overcometh and keepeth my works *unto the end*, to him will I give power over the nations: And he shall rule them with a rod of iron; as the vessels of a potter shall they be broken to shivers: even as I received of my father. And I will give him the morning star." We shall rule with him over the nations. That tells me a couple of things. Note again this notion of enduring or "keeping my works" *unto the end*. It is clearly implied that those who do not keep his works unto the end will not enjoy this power over the nations. Also in here is another hint that we shall rule and reign with Jesus in the millennium (which we will learn more about from Revelation 20). And it also tells me there will be mortals, "nations," yet alive on the earth. I don't know what the morning star represents, but I like the sound of it.

Chapter 3, verse 5: "He that overcometh, the same shall be clothed in white raiment; and I will not blot out his name out of the book of life, but I will confess his name before my Father, and before his angels." In order for a name to be blotted out of the book of life, it must first be written into the book. Some would suggest that all names are written in the book when they are born. But Revelation 13:8 has text that suggests that some names "are not written in the book of life." Then there is Revelation 17:8 which speaks of those whose, "names were not written in the book of life from the foundation of the world." So I don't think we can assume that all names are written in the book to start with. And if a name can be blotted out of the book, then this agrees with other texts such as, "He that endures to the end shall be saved." (Matt. 24:13) and suggests that salvation is not "once saved always saved." But rather it is entirely possible for a person to have come to the saving knowledge of Christ, and yet turn from his

105

faith under the threat of persecution or trials. This is why it is so important for us to build the foundations of our faith, so it will stand in the day of trouble.

Chapter 3, verses 10-12: "Because thou hast kept the word of my patience, I also will keep thee from the hour of temptation, which shall come upon all the world, to try them that dwell upon the earth. Behold, I come quickly: hold that fast which thou hast, that no man take thy crown." First, you have to have a crown before anyone can take it, and if it could not be taken, then this warning would not be necessary. Clearly we must hold fast to our faith. And just as clearly, the foundations of our faith will be tested to the max.

But we also need to speak to this statement, "I also will keep thee from the hour of temptation." This verse, along with Luke 21:36 which says, "Watch ye therefore, and pray always that ye may be accounted worthy to escape all these things that shall come to pass…" are often used to justify a "pre-tribulation rapture" position, which claims that the rapture will occur at the beginning of the 70th week of Daniel. In other words, there are those that assuredly believe that the church will be raptured out at the beginning of this seven year period and thus will not have to endure the tribulations that are prophesied during this time. This is an excellent example of how prophecy is often stretched to support ideas invented by men rather than allowing prophecy to speak for itself. Though it is clear from these two verses that there may be ways the Lord intends to allow some of his people to be protected or hidden or taken out by death or other means, these verses by themselves in no way indicate any rapture at all, much less when that rapture is to take place. And the assumption of a pre-seven year period rapture completely ignores (isolates this idea from) the larger body of information and direct revelation that the saints will be persecuted during this time (for which they must be present) and that the only "gathering" of the saints spoken of by any prophet (including Jesus) occurs at the end as Jesus is coming in the clouds of heaven. We will yet find even more evidence that the rapture occurs at the end of the tribulation in the epistles of the New Testament. But there are no scriptures anywhere that say anything about a gathering of the saints of any kind at any other time. Thus I am at a loss to understand why there is any controversy on this subject. As mentioned before, I will outline all the verses relating to the rapture in detail and in one place at the end of this book.

Chapter 3, verses 20-21: "Behold, I stand at the door and knock: if any man hear my voice, and open the door, I will come in to him, and will sup with him, and he with me. To him that overcometh will I grant to sit with me in my throne, even as I also overcame, and am set down with my Father in his throne." To sit with him in his throne is to rule with him. This is another hint as to how we will rule and reign with Jesus in the millennial period following his return.

After reading chapters four and five, we at last come to chapter 6 where the lamb that was slain begins to open the seals of the book. It will be fascinating to note as we start through the seals that these events appear to match up with the events described by Jesus in the gospels, and appear to focus on the last three and a half years, which is the great tribulation and the times of the gentiles. I've added these events to the timeline in figure 9 below so we can see how clearly they match.

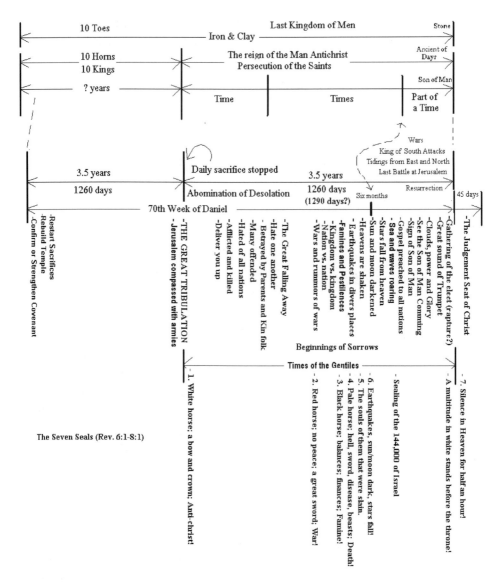

Figure 9: The Seven Seals of Revelation 6 and 7

So let's go through them:

Verse 2: The first seal: A white horse, a bow, a crown and the rider went forth conquering and to conquer. Many commentaries suggest this is Christ. I have no idea why other than it's a white horse, which Jesus is seen riding on in Revelation 19:11. There he is identified as King of kings and Lord of lords. Here there are no other identifying texts. All of the other horses and riders fit perfectly with the framework of events in the great tribulation period. If the white horse and rider represent Christ, it is out of place and confusing. But if we see the bow and crown as indicative of the authority of the man antichrist, and place him at the beginning of the great tribulation, then the picture and the symbolism fit perfectly into the timeline. It is my belief that this first rider does in fact represent the man antichrist.

Verse 4: The second seal: The red horse. This one takes peace from the earth and causes people to kill one another. This is war and rumors of war. It aligns perfectly with the timeline of kingdom against kingdom and nation against nation. One curious thing about this verse is the "great sword." There has been much speculation as to what this might be. Nuclear bombs? Laser weapons? H.A.A.R.P. (Look it up.) Who knows? There may yet be a new weapon we have not even heard of.

Verse 5: The third seal: The black horse. The balances represent the market place where things are bought and sold. There will, no doubt, be financial woes and difficulties. Verse 6 speaks of a days wage for just a measure of food. That means famine and starvation are occurring. I suspect there is some spiritual significance to the statement, "...and see thou hurt not the oil and the wine." But I would be speculating at best to suggest a meaning. At the least this seal represents global financial difficulties and very likely famine. Indeed, we see these events already looming on the horizon.

Verse 7: The fourth seal: The pale horse. This one seems to pull it all together under the name, "Death." Hell seems to be another "being" that is following after him to pick up the souls. The word here translated "hell" is actually the word "Hades" which represents the holding place for the unredeemed dead. They don't actually go to "hell," which is the Lake of Fire, until the judgment day at the end of all things (Revelation 20). But these two, Death and Hades, are given power over a fourth part of all the earth to kill with sword (war), hunger (famine), death (pestilence) and beasts of the earth (no safe place to hide from the wilderness.)

Verse 9: The fifth seal: At this point John sees the souls of many that were slain in the persecutions for their testimonies of God. They are standing before the throne of God asking him how long it will be before he finally comes to avenge them. They are given white robes and told to wait a little while until their fellow servants and brethren that are to be killed as they were should be fulfilled. There are going to be many martyrs. There just doesn't seem to be any way around it. He that has ears to hear, let him hear.

Verse 12: The sixth seal: Now the powers of heaven are shaken, just as in our timeline. The sun is darkened and the moon turns blood red. The stars fall from heaven and there is a great earthquake so that every mountain and island is moved out of its place. This is big stuff happening to the earth and heavens. The events will be so catastrophic that the kings and great men of the earth simply will not know what to do, and they will hide themselves in caves and dens of the earth to escape. Verses 16 and 17 suggest that these men will know that this is the great and terrible day of the wrath of the Lamb.

As we start chapter 7, keep in mind that we are still in the sixth seal. The seventh seal doesn't get opened until chapter 8 verse 1. So now John sees four angels standing on the four corners of the earth holding back the four winds. The "angels," the "four corners of the earth" and the "four winds" are symbolic pictures in the vision for what is happening on the earth. But the result is that there is no wind on the earth. That part, I would say is literal. Wind is caused by the uneven heating of the surface of the planet which creates high and low pressure zones. The air wants to move from the high pressure zones to the low pressure zones. Normally you would expect the air to move in a straight line from high to low, but because of the rotation of the planet there is something called the coriolis affect. The coriolis affect causes the wind to bend or curve around the high or low pressure zone in a spiral like fashion as it moves. The same affect is what makes the water going down the bathtub drain spiral into a tornado like shape. Low pressure zones rotate counter clockwise while high pressure zones rotate clockwise in the northern hemisphere of the globe. In the southern hemisphere it is the opposite. At any rate, when these astronomical events occur on the earth, it sounds like at least for a time there will be no wind, which would suggest there is no uneven heating, which would suggest the energy from the sun is not coming from just one direction anymore.

Chapter 7, verses 3 through 8: The hundred and forty four thousand. This is a bit of a mystery. We are only given limited information about these beings. In verses 2 and 3, John's vision records the angel with the seal of the living God telling the four angels who had power to hurt the earth and the sea to hold off until he had sealed the "servants of our God in their foreheads." This language suggests that these servants are on the earth and mortals. But we will find text later in Revelation that seems to blur that distinction.

In verse 4 John says he heard the number of those that were sealed, but then says there were 144,000 sealed of all the tribes of Israel. Now I don't want to try to pull more out of this text than is there, but given the text of verse 4 there is no reason to say that only these 144,000 were sealed. It does say that 144,000 were sealed of Israel, but it does not say that no others were sealed. Verse 3 says, "…until we have sealed the servants of our God in their foreheads." John says in verse 4 that he heard the number of them that were sealed. Then he says how many of those were of Israel. That's all he says. He does not say there are no others. I know it sounds like I'm trying to reach for something here but there is a reason why I am making this distinction. I will be discussing more on this when we get to Revelation 14 where we find some additional verses about the 144,000.

One interesting thing to note here is that in verse 6, Manasses, the son of Joseph, is listed as one of the twelve tribes of Israel that are numbered, while Dan is omitted. I have no idea the significance of this, but there it is.

The only thing we can get from this for our timeline is that this occurs just following the catastrophic astronomical upset of the heavens. So that places us nearer the end of the tribulation time.

Verse 9: This verse is very interesting because in chapter 6 verse 9, when the fifth seal was opened, he saw souls that were slain for the word of God crying out for vengeance. But suddenly here he sees "…a great multitude which no man could number of all nations, and kindreds, and people, and tongues…" standing before the throne in white robes with palms in their hands. Without the framework of Daniel and the details of Jesus in the gospels about this time, we might miss the fact that this sudden multitude of souls before the throne occurs in the timeline at the same time the "gathering of the elect" was to occur. But with that framework it becomes apparent that this is another reference to that great gathering or rapture of the saints. It all fits perfectly into the timeline without any stretching, massaging or manipulation of prophecy. And what will we be doing at that time? We will be praising and worshiping God just as is described in verses 10 through 12.

In verse 13 one of the elders in the vision asked John who these saints in white were, and where did they come from. It's interesting that the Father had those questions asked in the vision. Apparently John wasn't asking the questions the Father wanted to answer, so he had them asked by one of the elders. John wisely answers the elder, "Thou knowest." And in verse 14 we learn that "These are they which came out of *great tribulation* (the last 3.5 years) and have washed their robes and made them white in the blood of the Lamb." It would appear that this is not a general reference to the whole church or those that died in the Lord before this time, but rather is exclusive to those who suffered through the great tribulation. They were probably added to the saints of the fifth seal, although it doesn't say that specifically. Verses 15 and on to the end of the chapter describe some of the wonderful benefits these saints will enjoy. There is nothing in these texts to suggest that these benefits are exclusive to those who came out of the great tribulation. But there are texts in the gospels where Jesus suggested some would receive a "great reward" (Luke 6:22-23) for their sufferings, which does seem to suggest some differing levels of reward. But that's another study for another time.

Chapter 8, verse 1: This verse should have been tacked on to the end of chapter 7 rather than used to start chapter 8 because it records the last of the seven seals. All it says is that there was "silence in heaven for half an hour." I noted in my bible margin, "Peace at last." Whether this text suggests there *will* be silence in heaven after these events, or whether John was simply observing during his receiving of the vision that there was silence *in the vision* for half an hour, I don't know. I don't think it particularly matters. The key point is just that this event lines up perfectly in our timeline with Jesus now being on the earth as King and on his Throne.

With verse 2 of chapter 8, the vision resets and starts into another revelation of the end times from another perspective. But that's the topic of my next chapter.

9. The Seven Trumpets: Revelation Chapters 8 through 11

You should read Revelation chapters 8 through 11 before studying this chapter.

The seven trumpets, just like the seven seals, represent seven distinct events that are to occur during the last days. But this time the descriptions are more cryptic and symbolic. It is much more difficult with the trumpets to determine what is literal and what is representative of the events discussed. But we can still get a good general idea of what's happening and there are very clear clues as to where in the timeline these events fall.

Just to help give you the picture, I'm going to say up front that these events appear to occur just following or just preceding the major astronomical calamities of the sun and moon going dark and the stars falling from heaven. The reason for this claim will be shown later, but if you have that understanding in your mind going in it will help you visualize where in the timeline of events we are. It is also important to note that there is no way to know if the first four of these events follow one after another or if they happen somewhat simultaneously. Perhaps they occur one at a time in order over a period of time or perhaps they occur very close together over a period of time or perhaps they overlap and occur rapidly at about the same time. There is no text to guide us here. But there are indications to suggest that the last three trumpets occur sometime after the first four, and that these mark individual events in succession.

Chapter 8, verses 2 through 5: Seven trumpets were given to seven angels. But before they sounded there was another angel that was given much incense which was offered up "with the prayers of all saints" upon the alter. The smoke of the incense, which was with the prayers of the saints, rose up before the throne of God.

I'm not certain, but I believe these verses are used by some to suggest the necessity of prayer by the saints to usher in the return of Christ. There is a huge movement around the world that is attempting to coordinate 24 hour prayer from thousands of locations with the belief that this is necessary to usher in the return of Christ. Though I have no objection to prayer and believe in the effectiveness of the same, there is no scriptural basis to suggest it is up to us to do anything to make it possible for Jesus to come. He is coming whether we pray or not. But what these verses do tell us is that there will be a lot of prayer rising up before God at this time and that none of them are in vain.

Verse 7: And the first angel sounded. This was followed by hail, fire (lightning?) and "blood" being thrown onto the earth. Whether this is literal or symbolic, the result is said to be that a third part of the trees were burned up and all of the grass was burned up. Does it mean literally with fire like a forest fire, or does it mean from intense heat from the sun such as would be experienced if the sun went nova? Don't know. But we can say with some assurance that there is going to be a great destruction of foliage.

Verse 8: The second angel sounds. A great mountain burning with fire is cast into the sea and the sea becomes "blood." Is this a reference to a large meteorite or is it symbolic of something else? Does the sea literally become blood or is this symbolic of poison? Or does the "blood" just mean a lot of things die in the sea? It does say a third of all the life in the sea dies. But it can't just be that the water is poisoned because poison wouldn't destroy a third of all of the ships. That would take huge waves or a tsunami. Maybe it really is a huge asteroid or meteorite. It's hard to tell. Also, we don't know which "sea" is being referred to here. Is it one of the oceans, the Mediterranean Sea or perhaps the Sea of Galilee or the Dead Sea? There is nothing here to tell us.

Verse 10: The third angel sounds. Another great "star" falls from heaven burning like a lamp. Again, is it a literal meteorite or is it symbolic? This one "fell upon a third part of the rivers and upon the fountains of waters." It seems unlikely that a single meteorite from space could strike in so many different places so as to poison a third of the rivers and fountains of water. More likely this is representative of something else that causes many of the fresh water supplies of the earth to be poisoned. At the very least we know that the waters will be poisoned because they become "bitter" and many men die from them. The meaning of the word, "wormwood" doesn't add anything to our understanding. It basically just means the waters are poison. Some have suggested this carries the idea of radioactive poisoning, but I can't find any solid reason to assume that.

Verse 12: The fourth angel sounds. With this trumpet the sun is "smitten" by a third along with the moon and the stars so that the day shines not for a third of it and the night shines not for a third of it. This is a very clear picture of the rotation of the earth being increased so that the days are now only 16 hours long and no longer 24 hours. This also reinforces the statement made by Jesus in Matthew 24:22 that the "days shall be shortened."

At this point in the vision there is a break and John sees an angel flying through the midst of heaven crying out with a loud voice, "Woe, woe, woe." In Hebrew, when someone wishes to emphasize something as much as possible, they will repeat it three times. The point is being made that these last three trumpets are major catastrophic events for the people of the world.

Chapter 9, verse 1: The fifth angel sounds. Another "star" falls from heaven to the earth…but this time the "star" is called a "he" and is given a key to the bottomless pit. This makes it pretty clear that the "star" is symbolic language and also brings into question how we would interpret the "mountain" and the "stars" of the earlier trumpets. At the very least, this "star" represents something that opens up some terrible events. Whether or not the pit is a literal hole in the ground or a hole in the spirit realm, it is hard to say. But whatever else it is, it releases some terrible things called locusts that come forth to hurt men on the earth.

(Update, April 2019. You should do some research on the Large Hadron Collider built by CERN over in Europe. There is much speculation that this machine, if powered high enough, could punch a hole into "another dimension" with some concern that "beings" from that other dimension could pass through to our realm. Some speculate that it could create a black hole and destroy the earth. Others believe this could punch a hole into the spirit realm and allow demons to physically reenter our realm. There is a lot of controversy surrounding this structure, the statues that stand at its entrance and the opening ceremonies that celebrated its beginning. It is interesting to consider how a catastrophic event at this Collider could become the fulfillment of this prophecy.)

Verse 2: The smoke rose up and the sun and the air were darkened. This bothered me at first because I thought the sun was already darkened by this time. But when I remember that this stuff appears to be symbolic and representative of what's happening, rather than being literal descriptions of actual events, I am more comfortable. John is describing what he is seeing in the vision. What it represents I'm not sure. But whatever came out of that pit, it was thick and dark.

Verse 4: Now here is our first clue as to where this all fits in the timeline. The text says the "locusts" were not to hurt any plants or grass, but only those men which "have not the seal of God in their foreheads." This says the seal of God, placed on the foreheads of some men, had to already be in place. We learned that this occurred back in chapter 7 verse 3 during the sixth seal. The sixth seal was when there was a great earthquake and the sun and moon went dark and the stars fell from heaven (chap. 6, vss. 12-14). Then, in chapter 7 verse 3 the servants of God are sealed in their foreheads. Therefore, these events of the fifth trumpet have to be occurring after the events of the sixth seal.

I also must note here that we know there are at least 144,000 sealed from Israel, but the text of chapter 7 does not say that no others were sealed. The reason this is significant is because if we assume that only the 144,000 of Israel that were sealed are immune from the "hurt" caused by these locusts, then if there are any other "Christians" on the earth that have not the seal on their foreheads, they would technically be vulnerable. But if, as I believe is likely, all believers receive the seal when the 144,000 Israelis do, then all believers would be immune from this judgment. I admit here that all of this is rather murky and unclear. All I can say with certainty about this is that whatever God does, it will be the right thing.

Verse 5: Here is our next clue for the timeline. Verse 5 says that these "locusts" would not kill men, but just torment them for "five months." Well, I believe it is safe to assume that this torment will not continue beyond the return of Christ. Therefore, at the very least, the opening of the bottomless pit must occur some five months before the end of the period. If we give some leeway of time for the first four trumpets to occur and for the events of the sixth seal, which is the catastrophic astronomical stuff, to occur, we are now looking at about six months before the end of the seven years. This coincides with the six month point on our timeline suggested by the phrase, "Time, times and the dividing of time."

I said earlier that these points in the last three and a half years of the timeline that mark the beginning of the second year and the beginning of the last six months were not likely to be without reason. I believe it very likely that the major astronomical events described by Jesus in the gospels and now here in Revelation begin to occur at this last six month point. But this is just an entry in the Maybe Box.

Continuing on through verses 6 through 10 of chapter 9 and the events of the fifth trumpet, it is at least clear that these locusts, if they are indeed locusts and not actually representations of the weapons of modern warfare, are causing a lot of discomfort among the men of the earth. Once again in verse 10 the five months is mentioned. It just isn't really clear who or what these creatures represent. And those who say they know are not being intellectually honest.

Then in verse 11, we are told that these "locusts" have a king, who is the angel of the bottomless pit, and has the names Abaddon and Apollyon. Both of these names mean, "a destroyer" and are just other names for Satan. But the suggestion that the "locusts" have a king tends to suggest they may represent men and not just some kind of strange mindless insect.

Verse 12: One woe is past…two to go.

Verse 13: The sixth angel sounds. War! The descriptions of things John is seeing seem to clearly be describing modern warfare. The fire and brimstone and smoke coming from their "mouths" and the "tails" like serpents with heads on them sounds so much like tanks or artillery that it is hard to deny that this is what he is seeing. John says in verse 15 that a third of all men would be slain by these events.

Verses 14 through 16 speak of the four angels that were bound in the river Euphrates. At this point the text doesn't say anything about the river drying up, but in Revelation 16:12 it does. In Revelation 16:12 it says the river is dried up to prepare the way for the kings of the East. This could easily happen given the astronomical events that have just taken place. But this isn't mentioned here in chapter 9. Verse 16 then says John saw the number of the horsemen, which was 200 million. Many have combined chapter 9 and verse 16, with chapter 16 and verse 12, to suggest that the 200 million horsemen come from the East or China. I've even heard it suggested that China today, because of its one child per family policy and the resulting lack of women in their society, now boasts an army of 200 million. When I do the research on line, however, I don't find these numbers confirmed. Rather the number of military for China only comes up to around 7.5 million. That is far short of the 200 million to come from China as claimed by some groups.

But if you look at the texts separately, 16:12, simply says the Euphrates is dried up making the way for the kings of the East. No numbers are given for soldiers. 9:14 through 16 simply say the angels were bound in the Euphrates, no mention of the river drying up or the kings of the East. The number of horsemen was said to be 200 million. There is no suggestion that they all came from the east. More likely this number represents all the armies of all the nations of the world that are gathered together for the great slaughter of Armageddon.

But the results of these events of the sixth trumpet are clear. A third part of the men died and the rest repented not of their murders and sorceries, fornications and thefts. And they still worshiped the works of their own hands and idols of gold and silver and brass and stone and wood.

Chapter 10, verses 1 and 2: Another mighty angel appears. This one is clothed in a cloud and has a rainbow upon his head. His face is as bright as the sun and his feet as pillars of fire and he caries a little book open in his hand. He has one foot on the land and one foot on the sea. I have no idea what any of this means.

Verses 3-4: But when he cries out, seven thunders utter their voices. There were seven more key events or bits of information that John heard in this vision. Unfortunately, the angel told him to seal up what the thunders said and to not write them. Wow-wee, wouldn't you like to know what was in those thunders? I sure would. Unfortunately, there are no other scriptures anywhere that give any hints as to what these thunders were about. I have often wondered why they were even mentioned if we were not to know them. Perhaps there is still a revelation to be made someday to one of God's humble prophets. Or, perhaps it is simply better that we don't know everything that is to come. In any case, God sealed up their voices and the mystery is left to linger through the centuries.

Verses 5-7: This angel, that John is watching, now proclaims that there will be "time no longer." Other translations render this as "no more delay." Since I know there is to be a millennial reign on earth with mortals (which we will learn of in later chapters) I would say it is reasonable to assume that this statement is not intended to suggest time will cease to exist. I believe the angel is announcing that, "The time is up. The end has come. You had your chance. Now the King has come and the mystery of God is finished." What mystery? The same mystery that was revealed to God's servants the prophets, whom we have been studying here. That mystery is what is being revealed in this study. The mystery of Jesus the King and his Kingdom on earth.

Verses 8-11: There is not much revealed in these verses. It is simply shown that John must take this little book and prophesy again before many peoples, nations, tongues and kings. This he did and continues to do with the publication of his vision in the book of Revelation.

Chapter 11: We are still in the sixth trumpet here, but it is clear that the vision jumps back and gives some overview information covering the entire three and a half year period. It is in this chapter that we get confirmation that the "Times of the Gentiles" mentioned in Luke 21:24 do indeed coincide with the great tribulation or the last 3.5 years, and that there will be "two witnesses" also walking the earth during this entire time. Let's take a look.

Verses 1-2: The angel gives to John a reed and tells him to measure the temple, the alter and "them that worship therein." I have no idea of the significance of this. But he also tells him to leave out the outer court because it is "given unto the Gentiles: and the holy city shall they tread under foot forty and two months." "Tread under foot" is almost exactly the same as the words, "trodden down of the Gentiles" taken from Luke 21:24. This appears to be a reference to the same thing. In Luke it seems clear by the chronology of events given by Jesus, which is also confirmed by the accounts in Matthew 24 and Mark 13, that the "Times of the Gentiles" begins with the abomination of desolation, accomplished by the man antichrist, and ends with the return of Jesus at the end of the three and one half year period. Now in Revelation 11:2, we see the time of the Gentiles defined as lasting for 42 months. 42 months just so happens to equal…3.5 years.

There are those of the Dispensational persuasion that try to say the times of the Gentiles began with the destruction of the temple in 70 AD by the Romans, and ends with the rapture of the Church at the beginning of the 70th week of Daniel when God will supposedly again turn his attention back to the Jews almost exclusively. None of this is born out in the writings. It is, in my opinion, a fabrication of those who apparently wish to justify their assumptions. All one has to do is read the writings of the Bible without prejudice and the "Times of the Gentiles" becomes clearly obvious.

Verses 3-13 and the two witnesses: What a fascinating account. Apparently, there will be two "witnesses" that will give witness to Jesus Christ during the entire time of The Great Tribulation. Verse 3 says they will have power to prophesy 1,260 days clothed in sackcloth. 1,260 days is, once again, 3.5 Hebrew years. They are referred to in verse 4 as "the two olive trees and the two candlesticks standing before the God of the earth." Those descriptions don't give me any hints as to their identity. But in verse 6 they are described as those that, "...have power to shut heaven that it rain not *in the days of their prophecy*: and have power over waters to turn them to blood, and to smite the earth with all plagues as often as they will." Some believe, "in the days of their prophecy," speaks of the 3.5 years and the events described will happen during that time. But I believe this is a description of what these two men did when they were on the earth the first time. For it was Elijah in 1 Kings 17:1 that in the days of his prophecy shut up the heavens for three years that it did not rain. Paul also mentions this in James 5:17. And it was Moses, as we all know, in the book of Exodus, that turned the waters of the Nile into blood and brought all manner of plagues to the Egyptians until Pharaoh let the people of Israel go.

Elijah, as you may recall from 2 Kings 2:11, did not die but was caught up to heaven in a whirlwind and a chariot. Moses, on the other hand, according to Deuteronomy 34:5-6, died in the land of Moab and was buried. However, the text suggests he was buried by the Lord and no man knew the location of the sepulcher. Some have tried to suggest that the other "prophet" is most likely Enoch because in Genesis 5:24 it says that 'God took him" sort of like Elijah. And in Jude 15, Jude proclaims him a prophet. But there is no recorded history of Enoch turning water into blood or causing plagues on the earth. Besides, there is no "rule" that says in order for the two witnesses to come to the earth they had to be first "translated" rather than having died. There are numerous instances in the writings where people are "resurrected" from the dead. Why would we think it an amazing thing that Moses would be resurrected?

Rather than trying to insist on translation, let's just look at what is written. Rev. 11:6 says this witness had power to turn water into blood and smite the earth with plagues. That sounds like Moses. And it was Elijah and Moses that appeared to Jesus on the mount of transfiguration, not Elijah and Enoch. On the mount of transfiguration the voice of God spoke to the disciples and told them, "This is my beloved Son, hear him." This is recorded in Mark 9:7 and Luke 9:35. The significance of this was that Moses represented "the law" and Elijah represented "the prophets." These were the two major "witnesses" to the Israelites of the things concerning God. With Jesus present as "the son," God the Father was saying (my paraphrase), "Look, you've had the law and the prophets telling you about me. Now here is my very own beloved Son. *Listen to him!*" It is no stretch of the writings or the imagination to assume that these same two witnesses that were made manifest to the disciples at the mount of transfiguration, representing the law and the prophets, would once again be the two witnesses that will prophesy and give testimony to God and to Jesus during these last 3.5 years.

Apparently, these two "olive trees" are also mentioned in Zechariah 4. Verses 11-14 identify them as, "...the two anointed ones [sons of oil] that stand by the Lord of the whole earth." It would certainly seem likely that these are the same two olive trees, "...standing before the God of the earth" described in Revelation 11:4. It doesn't add anything to our understanding of the two witnesses but I wanted to point out the reference in Zechariah for completeness.

Also it should be noted that Malachi 3:1 says, "Behold, I will send my messenger, and he shall prepare the way before me..." And in Malachi 4:5 he says, "Behold, I will send you Elijah the prophet before the coming of the great and dreadful day of the Lord." These prophecies are why the disciples asked Jesus in Matthew 17:10, "Why then say the scribes that Elias must first come?" Jesus responds, "Elias truly shall first come, and restore all things." Then he goes on to explain that John the Baptist came in the Spirit and power of Elijah which fulfilled that prophecy for His first coming. But we know from this passage in Revelation 11 that at his second coming, Elijah will come not only in the Spirit and power of his prophecy but in bodily form as well. And this is truly the fulfillment of Malachi's prophecy because he says in Malachi 4:5, "Behold, I will send you Elijah the prophet *before the coming of the great and dreadful day of the Lord."* [Italics mine.] Jesus' first coming was not the great and dreadful day of the Lord, but his second coming certainly shall be.

Returning to Revelation 11, this story of the two witnesses also raises the question, are these two men the fulfillment of what Jesus said in Matthew 24:14 about the gospel being preached in all the world for a witness and in Revelation 14:6 about the angel having the everlasting gospel to preach unto them that dwell on the earth? These verses together with the story of the two witnesses all seem to agree with the idea that the Father is going to give the whole world one last chance to receive the truth about his Son Jesus, the King of Kings, before he destroys the world at his coming.

Verse 5: Whatever else these witnesses represent, they are two powerful dudes. It says here if any man would hurt them, fire proceeds out of their mouths and devours their enemies. I have a feeling the people of the world are not going to like these guys.

Verses 7-10: The devil from the bottomless pit, no doubt through his agents the man antichrist and the people of the political system antichrist, will make war with these two guys and eventually overcome them and kill them. They will be so afraid of them that they will not bury them but will leave their bodies in the street to rot. According to verse 8, this will happen in Jerusalem where also our Lord was crucified. They will be so happy at their deaths that they will send gifts to one another in celebration. Apparently, they will believe that they have won some great victory. But in their ignorance they fail to understand that the people of God never die. Not one hair of our heads will perish. (Luke 21:18)

Verses 11-14: "And after three days and a half, the Spirit of life from God entered into them and they stood upon their feet…" You cannot kill a servant of God. Moses gets resurrected for the second time in his life. (I don't know the significance of the number 3.5, but it sure appears a lot in end times prophecy.) As one would expect, the people of antichrist are terrified by this development. Then a beautiful thing happens. In verse 12 they hear a great voice from heaven saying to them, "Come up hither." Is that the call for the rapture? It happens right at that time in the timeline. Right at the end of the 3.5 years these two men are "raptured" up into heaven *in a cloud.* Are they the only two? Or does not this also coincide with the great deliverance of Daniel 12:1 and the "gathering of the elect" revealed by Jesus in Matthew 24:31, Mark 13:27 and Luke 21:28. Not to mention the multitudes before the throne at this time of the timeline as revealed in the Revelation 7:9 and the sixth seal. The evidence of the rapture being at this time in the timeline is overwhelming, and we haven't even looked at the confirming texts contained in the epistles. And I would be remiss if I did not point out once again the reference to "clouds" that are so often given in reference to the coming of King Jesus.

Verse 13: Now once this rapture occurs there is a great earthquake and a tenth part of Jerusalem will fall and some seven thousand men will perish. The rest will be afraid, and well they should be. For now the seventh angel is preparing to sound his trumpet blast, and the mystery of the Kingdom will be complete.

Verses 15-17: "And the seventh angel sounded..." and all was finished. The kingdoms of men are destroyed and become the kingdoms of our Lord and Christ. He shall reign for ever and ever, blessed be his name. And all of heaven celebrates and rejoices.

Verses 18-19: In these verses we once again get confirmation of the next event, which is the Judgment Seat of Christ. The sheep are separated from the goats as in Matthew 25 and the goats are judged. Then rewards are given to his servants the prophets and to the saints and to all them that fear his name. He will destroy those that destroyed the earth. In verse 19 the temple of heaven is opened. I don't know what this means. It may be a reference to the New Jerusalem which we are to learn about later or it may just be that John is relating scenes he is seeing in his vision of heaven. At any rate, there is a lot of stormy stuff going on in the vision. Perhaps this is significant of something or perhaps it is just a segue into the next part of the vision.

10. The Woman and the Dragon: Revelation Chapter 12

For this chapter, read chapter 12 of Revelation.

Now the vision takes a turn from focusing on smaller more specific events to step back and look at things from a broader perspective. The things described in this chapter are represented largely by symbolism but most of the symbols are explained in such a way as to make it obvious what they represent. Interspersed with these symbols are tidbits of information that are clearly literal. If we don't try to force the literal information into symbols, or force the symbols into something literal, but just take the text for what it is, I think it will be possible to draw much truth from this chapter.

In verses 1 and 2 we see a "great wonder in heaven," a woman clothed with the sun and the moon under her feet and on her head, "a crown of twelve stars." The stars are our first hint of who this woman represents. Our initial suspicion is that the twelve stars represent the twelve tribes of Israel or maybe even the twelve apostles. That is not explained here so at this point we don't know, but as we read through the chapter it soon becomes clear that this woman represents Israel. (Update 2017: A little further on I will explain that I now believe I may know what the 12 stars are all about.) In verse 2 we find she is pregnant and about to give birth. It seems fairly obvious that the child would be representative of Christ the King. Indeed, this is also confirmed later in the chapter.

But there is more of interest here than first meets the eye. In the heavens there is a constellation called Virgo. The word Virgo is Latin for, "Virgin." Virgo is a picture of a standing woman with an ear of wheat in her left hand and a branch in her right hand. When high in the Southern sky, she appears to be lying down sideways with her head to the right. And as the constellation sets in the West, she appears to dive head first into the ground. One of the "deacon" constellations grouped with Virgo is called Coma and depicts a picture of a virgin sitting and giving suck to a baby. So the picture of the sign of Virgo appears to speak of the virgin birth of Christ. (For more details on this subject check out the book God's Voice in the Stars by Kenneth C. Fleming.)

Now, the Hebrew calendar is not like ours. Their months follow the phases of the moon. Each new month begins when the priests first observe the sliver of the new moon as it follows the sun and sets on the Western horizon. The thing that is of interest here is that every year on the first day of the seventh month of the Jewish calendar, as the sun sets in the west and the priests are watching for the first sighting of the new moon, the sun is always somewhere inside of Virgo and the moon is always somewhere near her feet. So on that day she is essentially "clothed with the sun" and the moon is "under her feet." It's not quite that way every year, but close. And often it fits perfectly. The reason this is significant is because the first day of the seventh month is the Feast of Trumpets as established by God in Leviticus 23:24. There are 6 feasts established by God that the Jews were to keep every year. Three in the Spring and three in the Fall. The Spring feasts are Passover, First Fruits and Pentecost. The Fall feasts are Trumpets, the Day of Atonement, and Tabernacles. The first three feasts were fulfilled literally by Jesus on the feast days as he was crucified on Passover, rose from the dead on First Fruits and the Holy Ghost was poured out 50 days later on the day of Pentecost. The Fall feasts have never been fulfilled.

It is believed by many (including myself) that the Feast of Trumpets marks the day of the rapture as Christ returns with the great sound of a trumpet (Matt. 24:31). This is followed ten days later by the Day of Atonement which I believe represents the judgment seat of Christ, and 5 more days later, on the 15th, the Feast of Tabernacles. The Feast of Tabernacles is the feast, according to Zechariah 14:16-19 that all will be commanded to keep from year to year during the millennial reign of Christ. I believe this feast speaks of Christ the King who will then tabernacle among us on the earth and the celebration will most likely be to commemorate his return and the establishment of his throne.

Something very interesting about this relates to the words of Jesus in Matthew 24:36 where he said, "But of that day and hour knoweth no man." If the rapture is to occur on the first day of the seventh month you'd think we could figure out what that day is. But in reality, because of the way the first day of the month was determined in the Jewish culture in the days of Jesus (and probably will be again during those last years), we cannot. Today the beginnings of each month are determined scientifically based on astronomical calculations. But in Jesus' day, the first day of every month of the Jewish calendar was determined by when

125

the priest first *observed* the new moon. The new moon can only be seen shortly after sunset as the sky finally gets dark enough to see the long thin silver arc of the new moon which trails close behind the sun. If the moon is still too close to the sun so that it is not dark enough in the sky to see the moon before it sets, or if the sky happens to be cloudy that evening, the moon cannot be observed and the first day of the month will have to wait until the next day. Once the priest observes the moon, the exact hour of which is never known, he notifies the people and the trumpets are sounded marking the beginning of the month. This same procedure occurs on the seventh month, the first day of which is the Feast of Trumpets, as we discussed above. Therefore, no man knows the day or the hour that this will occur. But once the final seven years has begun, we can assuredly narrow it down to a very close proximity using the revelations of prophecy and the phases of the moon.

Now here is another interesting point to consider. If indeed the rapture is to occur at the Feast of Trumpets with Christ to return on or immediately after, and if this marks the end of the last seven years of Jewish history, then I believe we can safely assume that the beginning of that seven year period would also occur on or very near the feast day. Actually, if the last 7 years are 360 day years like all the other years of Daniel's 70 weeks, then the beginning of the period would be about 35 days *after* the feast. $365 - 360 = 5$. $5 \times 7 = 35$. Thus the last 7 prophetic years would be 35 days shorter than 7 solar years which would place the beginning of the period about a month after the Feast of Trumpets. If this is a reasonable assumption then we should pay special attention to events that occur around the October/November time frame of our calendar, watching for Israel to be given the right to exist or the freedom to once again build the temple and/or start the sacrificial rites of the old covenant, as we learned from Daniel 9:27 discussed earlier. We would also expect by this time that there would be some sort of world governance being headed by 10 kings or 10 principle directors.

(Update 2017: In January of this year, I learned something very interesting. It turns out that on September 23 of 2017, on or right after the Feast of Trumpets, Virgo will be very much clothed with the sun and the moon will be very much at her feet. But, what is interesting is, the planets Mercury, Mars and Venus will be lined up right under Leo and just to the left of the bright star Regulus, which is also in Leo. Leo appears just before Virgo, to her right, and just "above" her head.

126

It just so happens, that Leo has nine principle stars in the constellation. Those stars, plus the three planets, places a crown of twelve stars right over the head of Virgo. But that's not all. There is yet another significant event happening in Virgo at this time. Right now (February, 2017) the planet Jupiter is in the belly (the womb?) of Virgo and has been for about two months. Jupiter will "retrograde" (move backwards relative to the stars) while in the womb of Virgo, and thus will be there for 9 months from late December 2016 to late September 2017. After September 23, 2017, Jupiter will move on left, exiting between Virgo's legs, as if she had given birth to it.

This configuration of sun, moon and planets is extremely rare, occurring only once every 7,000 years or so. Thus, this configuration has never occurred in the 6,000 years of human history, and will not occur again for another 7,000 years, placing the next event far beyond what we expect the world to survive. That means September 23, 2017 is the only time in human history that Virgo will be clothed with the sun, the moon at her feet, having a crown of 12 stars over her head and having been "great with child" for 9 months to be delivered following that date. Amazing!

I originally believed verse 1 of chapter 12 was an obscure reference to the Feast of Trumpets when Jesus would return. But I am now inclined to believe this reference and this configuration of the stars and planets may be to mark the time when the 7 year period begins and not when it ends. This is especially likely given the texts that follow in Revelation chapter 12. The rest of the chapter concerns the man antichrist and events that occur during the 7 year period. It records Satan's fall to earth and his persecution of the saints.

Given this specific configuration of the stars on September 23, 2017, and the order in which events are listed in chapter 12, I am now seriously inclined to believe this may be marking the beginning of the final seven year period preceding Christ's return. We should pay special attention to world events this year to see if the other signs from Daniel which indicate the start of the 7 year period, which I mentioned just above, come to fruition.)

(Update 2019: September 23, 2017 came and went with no obvious consequence in the world. I did note a rather unusual spike in Sun activity that month, and there was a lot of buzz on the internet with people claiming that date was going to be the day of the rapture. Obviously that didn't happen. But the signs of the beginning of the final 7 year period also didn't happen. Basically…. nothing happened.)

Moving on, Revelation 12:3 gives us the picture of the great red dragon with seven heads and ten horns. It is clear from verse 9 that this dragon represents Satan, but it is also clear from the ten horns which correspond to the ten kings and ten horns of Daniel 7 that this represents the political system of antichrist. This one is a little different from Daniel's beast, however, in that it has seven heads. It is interesting to note here that on the heads are seven crowns. We are not told what the heads or the crowns represent. There is another beast that comes up from the sea in chapter 13 that also has seven heads and ten horns. But that is a different vision and in that vision it is the horns that have crowns, not the heads. So it may be that they have similar representations, clearly they both represent the political system of antichrist, but in this chapter with the dragon we are not told anywhere what the seven heads or the seven crowns represent. And anyone who says they know is not being intellectually honest.

It says in verse 4 that this dragon drew a third of the stars of heaven and cast them to the earth. It is just speculation on my part, but I have always assumed that these stars represent the angels that served Lucifer. My understanding from the writings is that there are three archangels, Michael, Gabriel and Lucifer. I've always believed that the archangels have some free will, otherwise Lucifer could not have made choices contrary to the will of God and fallen. I've always been of the opinion that the average rank and file angels do not have free will but are simply the messengers (which is what the word angel means) of God. If the angels are assigned to the archangels in the hierarchy of heaven, then when Lucifer fell his third of the angels would simply follow with him. I would point out that in 12:9 they are referred to as, "*his* angels." None of this really matters in terms of prophecy, but may be an interesting thought for you.

At any rate, this dragon now stands ready to devour the man child to be delivered by the woman. Satan wanted to destroy Jesus by causing him to serve him instead of God, as shown in the wilderness temptations described in Matthew 4 and Luke 4. But in the vision, just as in real life, when the Son was brought forth he was caught up unto God and to his throne.

Verse 6 says that the woman then fled into the wilderness where she has a *place prepared of God* where she will be fed for 1,260 days. There is our 3.5 years again. This also coincides with the narratives of Jesus in the gospels where he speaks of the abomination of desolation and how when they see this happening, or Jerusalem surrounded by armies, they should flee to the wilderness. Clearly there is some provision prepared by God to take care of some of the population of Israel. This may also be the fulfillment of the verses of Luke 21:36 where Jesus says to pray that you might be counted worthy to escape, and Revelation 3:10 where Jesus says, "Because you have kept the word of my patience, I also will keep you from the hour of temptation which shall come upon all the world to try them that dwell upon the earth." Many have attempted to use these verses to support the assumption of a pre-tribulation rapture. But that assumption has no clear basis in prophecy. There are no texts in the writings that speak of any kind of gathering of the saints prior to the coming of the King. But here is a clear description of protection and escape in Revelation 12:6, which clearly agrees with, and I believe should be embraced as explaining, Luke 21:36 and Revelation 3:10, rather than the manufactured idea of a pre-tribulation rapture. There are also other scriptures that speak of this protection and escape. Look at Zephaniah 2:3, Isaiah 33:15-16, Isaiah 26:20-21 and Isaiah 57:1. The last reference suggests escape by death, but all of the others speak clearly of being hidden away, fed and protected during the time of God's wrath. This is the real mystery of the end of days, not the idea of a pre-tribulation rapture.

Now here's an interesting speculation that sits squarely in the Maybe Box. This is purely speculation on my part and has no clear support of prophecy, but I have wondered if the United States might be the "place prepared by God" where a portion of His people escape to and are hid. It is a long stretch, I know. When you look at current events it appears that the US is on its way to being a third world country and just another victim of the new world order. But if, by chance, America was truly ordained of God to be one nation under God and has some real significance in God's plans for the end times, it is remotely possible that the people of the US will resist the actions of the world government, throw the bums out of office, and re-establish itself as a separate free nation. That would be wonderful. (Update 2017: It's interesting to note that with the election of Donald Trump to the presidency, there is a new nationalism in the US, and America seems to be pulling away from the idea of globalism. We'll see how this plays out. His resistance to globalism may actually be the catalyst that brings it about. All in the Maybe box.) I have little to base this idea on other than wishful thinking and a curiosity as to whether or not there is real spiritual significance to the Christian founding of this nation. But it is interesting to note in verse 14 that prophecy says, "And to the woman were given two wings of *a great eagle* that she might fly into the wilderness…" I don't want to make too much of the "eagle" thing. That would be a stretch. But I could easily envision a massive airlift from Israel to the US as the man antichrist moves into the area and surrounds Jerusalem. It's just a thought.

The Dispensationalist will say that the lost city of Petra is the place prepared by God to hide the remnant of Israel. There is a scripture in Isaiah 16:1-4, that suggests this idea. The word used in the KJV for Petra is "Sela." This is just another name for the city of Petra. And in verse 4 it says, "Let mine outcasts dwell with thee, Moab; be thou a covert to them from the face of the spoiler." Is this a veiled reference to a remnant being hidden away from the man antichrist? Perhaps. But there are also problems with this idea. First, Petra is not in Israel, but rather lies inside of Jordon, which is one of Israel's enemies. Jordon is not openly hostile to Israel these days, but they are a Muslim nation. And things can change rapidly. Second, Petra, though easily defendable in the days of horses and swords, is wide open to invasion and attack from the air. It would be vulnerable in the days of modern warfare to being over run. Of course, we cannot deny that the Lord, who prepared this place and brought his people to it, could also supernaturally defend it. So, one could certainly speculate on this idea of Petra. Unfortunately, the idea of Petra isn't presented as a speculation by the Dispensationalist. Rather it is presented and taught as a fact. This is not an intellectually honest approach to understanding Scripture.

Verse 7 begins to discuss the spiritual battle that is taking place in the heavens. Michael, one of the archangels along with *his* angels fights against the dragon and *his* angels. The dragon, of course, loses and is cast out in verse 9. Verse 9 is where we learn the identity of the dragon, the old serpent which is the Devil and Satan, which deceives the whole world.

Not much doubt about this one. But it also says *his* angels were cast out with him. It doesn't sound like the angels had any choice in the matter.

At this point, verse 10, the Kingdom has come with the power of His Christ for the "accuser of our brethren is cast down..." Verse 11 is important because it tells us how we overcame him. It was by the blood of the lamb and by the word of our testimony. Don't ever underestimate the power of your personal testimony to overcome the devil in other people's lives. And finally, we loved not our lives unto death. He that endures to the end shall be saved. He that does not, will not. The truth of this is everywhere in the writings of the Bible. Authentic Christianity will cost you. Perhaps even your very life. Though there is also a constant underlying foundation of joy along the way, if your faith in Christ has not cost you something, I question its authenticity.

So now, in verse 12, the heavens are rejoicing but those on the earth are in big trouble because the devil has come down to them and he is mad knowing he has but a short time. The prophecy makes it clear that this event occurs right at the time of the arising of the man antichrist and the abomination of desolation. This is seen in verse 13 which describes how, when he sees that he has been cast out of heaven to the earth, he begins to persecute the woman.   Jesus made it clear in the gospels that this was the time to flee Jerusalem, which coincides with verse 14 where the woman is given wings to flee into the wilderness, and the time of the abomination of desolation.

In verse 14 it says that the woman was carried away into "her place" which we learned in verse 6 was prepared for her by God, to be "nourished," which means fed and taken care of, "for a time, and times, and half a time, from the face of the serpent." The word for "time" here means "an occasion," which, just as the Hebrew word in Daniel, suggests an annual event, or by inference, a year. Once again, we have the three and a half year period measured out.

In verse 15, the serpent tries to "drown" her with a flood but God helps her escape to her place of hiding by opening up the earth and swallowing the water. These things are probably symbolic of something else but the intent of Satan and the antichrist is obvious. Since the woman is carried away and hid at this time, and we know from all the other prophecies on the timeline that this happens at the abomination of desolation, we also know that the time Satan will be cast out with his angels is this time.

Verse 17 also confirms this as it describes how, in his frustration at not being able to get the woman, he then turns his wrath on those who keep the commandments of God and have the testimony of Jesus Christ. This would be the Church and coincides with all of the prophecies going before of the great persecution from the man antichrist. This might also be another veiled reference to the United States. Though I know there are Christians all over the world, the current attitude of the Muslim nations is that Israel is the little Satan and America is the great Satan. When the man antichrist tries to get to the Jews that are fleeing (assuming to America) and fails, his anger would then be turned onto the "Great Satan" of America. It's just another interesting thought. But from these verses I believe we can conclude that the man antichrist will be the embodiment of and possessed by Satan himself.

11. The Beast and the False Prophet: Revelation Chapter 13

For this chapter, read chapter 13 of Revelation.

Now in chapter 13 another whole new vision begins. This one starts with John standing on the sands of the sea and a beast rises up from the sea. This one also has seven heads and ten horns, but unlike the dragon of chapter 12, it is the horns on this beast that have the crowns. Also on this beast the heads have the name of blasphemy. It is significant that the beast comes up out of the sea. The sea in prophetic language almost always represents the sea of people as shown in Revelation 17:15. So putting this all together, it is very clear that this beast represents the political system of antichrist. Many people refer to the beast and the man antichrist interchangeably. This is not accurate. In Daniel, the beast with 10 horns represented the political system and the little horn represented the man antichrist. The same is true here. The beast is the system, not just the man antichrist, and is made up of many, many people.

Verse 2 shows us that the beast appeared to be made of many different animals. This would suggest to me the inclusion of many different nations or peoples in this political system. But I would be remiss if I failed to point out that in Daniel 7:4-6 Babylon is referred to as like a lion, the Meads and Persians like a bear and the Greeks as a leopard. Each kingdom of man fed into the next building the beast, the political system of antichrist. But it is from the dragon, which is Satan, that this system derives its great power and authority.

Verse 3: This is an intriguing verse. One of the heads of the beast is wounded unto death but miraculously survives. Since this is a political system and not just a single man, I don't exactly know what this will represent. We don't really know what the heads represent. Later, in chapter 17 John has another vision with a beast with seven heads and 10 horns. In this vision the heads are said to be seven mountains. But we don't know if we can carry that interpretation back to this beast. At best, since we know this beast represents the political system and not just a man, we might speculate that there is some sort of blow to one of the major segments of this system. Most would have expected this segment to perish but somehow it survives which amazes everyone and gives them greater awe and confidence in this new world system. But the prophecies are not real clear here on this point. All we know is that something major is going to happen to some part of the system, the survival of which will amaze and mesmerize the world. Also, it appears that this event occurs during the reign of the 10 kings and before the man antichrist comes on the scene. I say this because this wounding is described in verses 3 and 4 and it is not until verse 5 that the "mouth speaking great things and blasphemies" appears to come on the scene.

Now there are those who blindly claim from these prophecies that the man antichrist will be shot in the head but miraculously survive. These claimants are not only being intellectually dishonest with the writings but incredibly imaginative. Only one of the seven heads is wounded. And we know that it is not the heads but the horns that represent kings or rulers, of which the man antichrist is just a little horn that comes up later. In fact, as I mentioned above, the man antichrist does not come on the scene until verse 5. There is no logical or reasonable basis for this claim of a gunshot wound to the head of the man antichrist.

Verse 4: This system will appear to be so amazing, or at least will be presented as so amazing by propaganda that people will not only respect it but will worship it. It will become more than just a political system or governmental authority, but will be a religious type entity that people will begin to worship. Perhaps they will be required to worship it. Perhaps it will have more of an Islamic face rather than a European face. But everyone will be amazed at its power and authority and may actually feel safe believing that no one could possibly make war with this system, the beast. They will be saying, "Who is able to make war with him?" I don't know if this is an expression of pride or of fear. But this seems to suggest that the "wound" has something to do with a battle or an attack on the new world order of antichrist.

Now in verse 5, we see the emergence of the man antichrist. This is the "mouth" speaking great things and blasphemies. *He* was given power to continue 42 months. I believe the "he" spoken of here is the mouth, which represents the man antichrist, because we know that the last kingdom of men, which is the political system of antichrist, begins before the man antichrist enters onto the scene. Thus it must be the "mouth" that is given power to continue 42 months. How long is 42 months? 3.5 years.

Verse 6: As we've heard before of the man antichrist, he opened his mouth in blasphemy against God to blaspheme his name and his tabernacle (which today does not exist) and those that dwell in heaven. This guy is totally anti heaven and anti Christ. He is full of the devil that was cast out of heaven in chapter 12 verse 9.

Verses 7-8: Just as we learned in Daniel 7:21-22, this man antichrist along with the beast or political system antichrist will make war with the saints and overcome them. This is a sad but true thing. Many will be tried and made white. As with the Hebrew, the word for saints here means, "holy ones." The theme of the persecution of the saints during the last 3.5 years is seen over and over again. And in this verse we see that the man antichrist is given power over all kindreds, tongues and nations. All the world will worship him whose names are not written in the Lamb's book of life. This is one of those books mentioned in Daniel 7 verse 10. It is the book of life of the Lamb slain from the foundation of the world.

"Slain from the foundation of the world." Just a side note, but writings make it clear that the plan of salvation for mankind through the cross of Christ was God's intention from the very beginning of creation.

Now in verse 9 we get this statement, "If any man have an ear, let him hear." I don't think this statement is being used to emphasize what came in the verses before it. Rather, I believe the writer or speaker is attempting to get the reader's attention to focus on the text that is to follow in verse 10.

Verse 10 is an important instruction from the Lord. Modern translations try to explain what this means as those who are to die by the sword will do so, and those who are to go into captivity will do so. "Que sera sera." Whatever will be will be. But that is a distortion of the text. What it is saying is, if you try to fight the antichrist using the conventional means of weapons at your disposal, you will lose. In other words, if you take up a sword or a weapon you will die by a sword or weapon. If you take prisoners you yourself will be taken prisoner. This, of course, will be frustrating because many saints will feel like we should physically fight. And it will try our patience. But remember the words of Jesus as he stood before Pilate in John 18:36, "…If my kingdom were of this world, then would my servants fight…but now is my kingdom not from hence." Our kingdom is already won and secured. We have nothing to fight for here.

135

If we must fight it would be against Satan in the lives of those around us as we seek to save the lost. For we fight not against flesh and blood (Ephesians 6:12). The wars on the earth are not our battles. But the battle for the souls of men always continues.

Verse 11: Then the vision continues with the emergence of another beast. This one comes up out of the earth, the significance of which I am not sure. But at the least he is masquerading as Jesus the lamb that was slain, for he has two horns like a lamb. But he speaks as the dragon and gets his power from the dragon. He will appear as an "angel of light." (2 Cor. 11:14) But you will be able to discern who and what he is by his attitude, by the way he speaks (because he speaks as a dragon) and the spirit through which he operates. This guy is commonly referred to as the "false prophet" because of Revelation 16:13, 19:20 and 20:10.

Verse 12: Since this guy exercises all of the power of the first beast and causes all to worship the first beast, which is the political system of antichrist now headed up by the man antichrist, there is some question as to whether this new beast, the false prophet, is a man or an organization. Chances are good that it is more than just a man. But whatever he is, he uses the fact that one of the heads of the first beast was wounded and healed as leverage to cause people to worship the first beast.

Verses 13-18: Now this false prophet, whether man or organization, will have power to do amazing miracles and signs and wonders in the sight of men. Will he do them in the name of Jesus? Jesus did warn us of such false prophets doing false signs and wonders in the name of Jesus. It may be very possible that the evil political system of antichrist will attempt to hijack the name of Jesus for its own purposes and suppose to convince people that here is the great power of Jesus. Jesus warned us of this. Don't believe them.

An interesting note: I have learned that Islam does not deny the existence of Jesus. In fact, they prophesy that he will return with the twelfth Imam or the Mahdi. But they say Jesus was not the son of God but only a prophet and will tell people when he comes that they should reject Christianity and turn to Islam. In other words, he will cause the people to worship Islam and the Mahdi. Could this be the fulfillment of the false prophet?

One of the things that this false prophet is going to do is to have an image made to the beast. Here is where some of the confusion comes in giving people the idea that the beast is the man antichrist. The assumption is that the image will be a statue made to look like the man antichrist but there is nothing in the text on which to base that assumption. The image or "likeness" as it is defined in Strong's, is of the *beast*. Not of a man. The fact from verse 15 that the false prophet was able to give the image the power to speak, does not mean it has to be the image of a man. Many things can be made to speak, even inanimate objects. We must be very careful not to be so sure we understand what this is talking about. When we see it or hear it, we will know. But until then, this is very unclear.

Now, we should not leave verse 14 without noting that the beast that "had the wound" got that wound "by a sword." Whatever else that may stand for; it at least stands for some sort of weapon. It still doesn't explain what happened, but when it does happen in reality, I believe those who are alive to witness the event will then understand exactly what this is speaking of. Just keep in mind that it involves the beast, which is the whole political system, and not just a single man, the antichrist.

Ok, back to verse 15. Now things are getting really intense. Now you have to worship the beast and the image of the beast or you will be killed. Islam? This false prophet guy or group is really a bad dude. In verse 16 we see the infamous mark of the beast, 666. This mark is to be placed on the right hand or the forehead. It is by this that men buy and sell. This didn't make much sense to people at the time, but today we understand easily the concept of credit cards and electronic accounts. This number, which is the number of a man's name (which I believe refers to the name of the one that gets the mark not the name of the beast) will be the new credit card or account number that allows people to do commerce. Most likely, paper money will be a thing of the past and everything will be electronic. There is technology in existence today which allows a chip to be implanted under the skin that can communicate to terminals without actually coming into contact with them. This chip could be used for such transactions. Perhaps the "mark" is to show where the chip was inserted. Whether or not this is what this text is about remains to be seen. But clearly this mark will be intended to allow the beast to track and control all activities of the people. And the only way you will get the mark is by professing allegiance to and worshiping the beast and the image to the beast. This will be the reason why "taking the mark" will be so contrary to the faith of Christ.

Verse 18 is interesting but I don't believe we will understand the significance of the number 666 until the time comes. The verse starts out, "Here is wisdom" which, as I said before, means pay attention to what follows. "Let him that understands *count* the number of *the beast…*" It will only come to those who understand, to those who are thinking and looking for the solution to the riddle, to those who know these writings and are meditating on them. Part of the riddle is, to "count" or, according to Strong's dictionary it might mean, "to calculate" or "enumerate" the number. I'm not sure what that suggests but the wording is not by accident. Likely we won't understand until we see it, but keep this little clue in mind. The number must be *counted or calculated or enumerated.* It also says it is the number of the *beast*, not the man antichrist. Don't confuse the two. However, the picture is confused by the next statement, "…for it is the number of a man; and *his* number is 666." I really don't know quite what to make of this, but I believe the key to the riddle is in *counting* or *calculating* or could I say *computing* the number of the beast.

There is no shortage of theories, assumptions or speculations as to what this number means or who it stands for. Some ancient manuscripts write out the numbers 666 using the Greek words for six hundred sixty six. Some use just three Greek letters that are seen to represent 600, 60 and 6 respectively. Still other manuscripts suggest that the number is 616. There is a lot of disagreement on this. Many try to translate letters of people's names to numbers and add them up to 666. Dozens of names either in English or translated to Greek seem to fit the formula but none of them really make sense. Some point out that the first and last of the three Greek letters for this number are the same as the first and last letters for the word "Christ" while the middle letter looks like a serpent. Some say the three Greek letters were originally Arabic because when you flip the middle letter over diagonally, it looks like the Arabic word for Allah, and the first letter, Chi, looks like crossed swords, a symbol of Islam, and the last letter, stigma, looks like the Arabic word for "in the name of." (Arabic reads right to left.) Thus, they say, it spells, "In the name of Allah." Confusion and speculation abound.

Here is the main point. It doesn't matter. We already know so much detail surrounding the appearance of the man antichrist that when he appears on the scene and uproots three kings and attacks Jerusalem and sets up the abomination of desolation, there will be no questioning who he is regardless of any numbers. As for the mark, well, whatever it is or represents, don't take it. If 666 or 616 is a hint to help identify the mark, fine. We'll recognize it when it comes. But to get it you will have to worship the beast and the image to the beast. Don't do it. You will know what it is when the time comes. There will be no doubt.

12. Another Review of Events: Revelation Chapter 14:

For this chapter, read chapter 14 of Revelation.

Chapter 14 opens with Jesus, as a lamb, standing on mount Sion (Mt. Zion) and with him a hundred and forty four thousand, having his father's name written on their foreheads. At first blush one would think this is the same 144,000 spoken of in Revelation 7:4. It may well be but there is nothing other than the number and the fact that they are all sealed on their foreheads or have the Father's name on their foreheads, that they have in common. Some have suggested that this group is a separate group of 144,000 and may represent the church, while the first group represented Israel. Well we do know that the first group is taken from the twelve tribes of Israel, and no such distinction is made here in chapter 14. But when it comes to the redeemed of the Lord, I get a little uneasy when we start trying to separate the redeemed Jews from the redeemed Gentiles. In Christ we are all grafted into the same olive tree, which is Israel (Romans 11:17-24), and thus we, in essence, become a part of the true Israel. For not all that are of Israel are Israel, but those that are of the promise. The redeemed are spiritual Israel. (Romans 9:6-8) At the same time, however, there is a natural Israel consisting of the physical decedents of Jacob.

So, is this the same 144,000 as chapter 7? I don't know. Chances are good that it is. But to say that categorically would be to add something to prophecy that is not there.

Now in verses 2-3 John sees some things that suggest something is changing. There is a great voice like many waters and thunder and harpers harping. The clue is they sung a "new song" before the throne and the four beasts and the elders. I believe that means something new is happening. It also says that only the 144,000 could learn this song which means they have a unique mission or purpose. No other man fits this category.

One last interesting note from verse 3. It says the 144,000 were, "redeemed from the earth." This sure sounds like they are of the saved or of the Church. What we don't know is if they are still mortal men or if they have been resurrected. However, the timing of this in verse 1 places them with the Lamb which is now standing on Mt. Sion. Timing wise, this would place us beyond the rapture and the resurrection and thus, I would assume these to be men in their glorified bodies and not mortal men. And the words, "*from* the earth" are not lost on me.

Verses 4 and 5 give us more information about this 144,000. I should say up front that there are many that believe that the descriptions that follow are only symbolic in nature and give representation of the spiritual state of the church. After all, much of the visions of Revelation are just that, symbolic. This is perhaps true, but there is nothing here that makes that idea definite. So, following my rules of interpretation, unless it is obviously symbolic and representative of something else, I take the words literally for what they say. Either way, the 144,000 are a bit of a mystery and we may never know exactly what or who they represent until the time they are revealed.

But, assuming the texts should be taken literally, verse 4 says they are not defiled with women but are virgins. First, this suggests that they are all men. I'm not sure what this would say if it were just a symbolic representation of the Church. Then it says, "these are they that follow the lamb withersoever he goeth." That would work for the Church, but also works literally for an army that is following Christ as he purges the world of all evil men. Then it says, "These were redeemed from among men, being the first fruits unto God and to the Lamb." Well, that statement could hardly be taken as symbolic or representative. It seems to be a literal description of some men who are redeemed of the earth. The first thing that is pointed out by those who propose this as a second group of 144,000 is that it says they were redeemed from among, "men." In chapter 7 it says they were of Israel. Whether this is a significant distinction or not is hard to tell, for the 144,000 of Israel would also be redeemed from among men. The second thing we get from this is that these 144,000 are not the whole harvest, but only the "first fruits" of the harvest. The first fruits was the part of the harvest that was taken out of the field first, and usually represented the tithe to the Lord. (2 Chronicles 31:5) The key point to see here is that the "first fruits" are not the whole harvest. Therefore, these 144,000 do not represent the whole of the redeemed. Lastly, "first fruits" usually refers to what is harvested…well…first. Revelation 7 suggests that these were marked on their foreheads while still here on the earth as men, which would place them in the last days and far from being the first men redeemed from the earth. Again, perhaps that group is just from Israel, and this group is made up of some of the first Christians of the ages. It's confusing and not at all clear. Basically we just have to leave this where it is and say we just don't have enough information to understand clearly who or what the 144,000 represent. Those who do claim to know are not being intellectually honest. But such understanding is not vital to our understanding of the timeline.

Verse 5 says, "in their mouth was found no guile:" which means they never lie nor deceive "for they are without fault before the throne of God." Whatever else this means, God at least sees them as faultless. This is, no doubt, the result of the cross of Christ, for there is no man redeemed from the face of the earth that has not sinned. (Romans 3:23)

Regardless, this is all we know of the 144,000. The only other time we even see the number 144 in the Bible is in Revelation 21 when the walls of the city are measured at 144 cubits. So if there is any prophetic significance to the number 144, it is no where else to be found in the writngs. It might also be interesting to note, if you are into numerology, that 12 x 12 = 144. I have no idea what that means…if anything.

Verses 6 and 7 change the subject and the vision continues with another angel coming and proclaiming the everlasting gospel to preach unto them that dwell on the earth, and to every nation and kindred and tongue and people. Verse 7 tells you what the angel is preaching. As I mentioned earlier, if you go back to Matthew 24:14 and read Jesus' prophecy that the gospel of the kingdom would be preached to all the world just before the end comes, you quickly see that this event in Revelation 14:6-7 is the fulfillment of that prophecy.

Now verse 6 says it was an angel flying in the midst of heaven. It is entirely possible that this could be literal since many strange spiritual things will be happening during this time, such as the two witnesses, Moses and Elijah. But as I have speculated earlier, it could be that Moses and Elijah are the fulfillment of this prophecy as their whole mission during the last 3.5 years is to be "witnesses" to Christ and the Kingdom. Their ministry, as described in Revelation 11, is to be "witnesses" and to "prophesy" (vs. 3) and to give "testimony" (vs. 7). Whether it is these two, or an angel, God is giving the world one last chance to receive him and to turn from their wicked ways before he comes to destroy the wicked.

Verse 8: Then another angel comes along proclaiming that Babylon is fallen, is fallen. We will learn in chapter 17 of Revelation who Babylon is and what that "city" represents. Just keep in mind that Babylon represented the beginning of the man made kingdoms that would rule the world instead of Christ, the kingdoms of antichrist. Therefore, the name "Babylon" could be used to represent the entirety of all of the man made kingdoms of antichrist. We will also learn in chapters 17 and 18 that she represents the beginnings of man's monetary system and the evils and woes that come of it. Basically, I believe verse 8 is a reference to the collapse of the man made monetary system as well as the man made kingdom of antichrist.

Some use this verse and others like it in chapters 17 and 18 to suggest that the literal city of Babylon must be rebuilt with its magnificent walls and hanging gardens. After all, "that great city" cannot fall if it is not first rebuilt. Right? But when we get to Revelation 17 and 18, I believe we will find ample evidence that this is a spiritual or symbolic representation of the beginnings of the kingdoms of men and the beginnings of the world banking and monetary system and cannot simply represent a solitary city. For what it's worth, the old city of Babylon today is little more than a huge sandy heap of rubble in the desert. It would take many, many years to turn it into any kind of meaningful city.

In verses 9 through 11, a third angel comes and announces the dangers of worshiping the beast, the political system of antichrist, or the image of the beast and of receiving the mark. Clearly, the only way you will get this mark in your hand or forehead is if you worship the beast. It will require some sort of statement of allegiance to the beast and that is why all such who do so will drink of the wine of the wrath of God. It will not be a fun time for these folks.

It is not insignificant that the requirement to participate in this new monetary system, using the mark of the beast (v. 9), appears to follow on the heels of the fall of Babylon (v. 8), which I believe and we will learn later represents the current world monetary system of banking.

As we learned in chapter 13, the mark of the beast will be necessary to buy and sell anything. I'm sure that would include food. Those who have not the mark will not be able to participate in any form of commerce. Thus, verse 12, "Here is the patience of the saints: here are they that keep the commandments of God and the faith of Jesus." Christians will not have the mark to buy food or any other necessity. We will be totally dependent on the Father for our provision. That will take a lot of faith…and a lot of patience. Are you ready?

So…if that wasn't bad enough, now we get to verse 13. "Blessed are the dead which die in the Lord from henceforth…that they may rest from their labors…" These will be dark days. So dark that they will say those who die in the Lord are more blessed then those that still live. Yet, as the redeemed, we know that we never really die. Rather we just go on to our reward, "…and their works do follow them." In other words, our faithfulness unto death will not be forgotten in heaven. But for those who are left, if they know the words of this book and have watched the events of the world unfold, they will also know that the time is soon for them to look up, for their redemption draws near.

In fact, starting in verse 14, we see our Lord, the Son of man, coming on a cloud, just as described in numerous prophecies referring to his return, with a gold crown on his head. He thrusts in his sickle and in verse 16 we read that, "the earth is reaped." This is another clear reference to the rapture. For only the redeemed of the earth will be reaped by the Son of Man.

After Him, in verse 17, another angel comes with another sickle and reaps another harvest of souls. Except, this harvest is thrown into the great wine press of the wrath of God. This is, no doubt, a reference to that last great battle, the battle of Armageddon, where the blood will run to the depth of the horses' bridles for a space of 1600 furlongs. Generally, a furlong is described as being about an eighth of a mile. If that is true, this would be a distance of some 200 miles which, by the way, is the approximate North/South length of the nation of Israel today.

13. The Seven Last Plagues: Revelation Chapters 15 and 16

For this chapter, read chapters 15 and 16 of Revelation.

Chapter 15 starts off with John seeing a great and marvelous sign in heaven, seven angels having the seven last plagues which fill up the wrath of God. Many say these days that when earthquakes and disasters happen they are not the judgments of God, but rather just random events of chance. But this verse makes it pretty clear that the plagues to follow are not random chance or just the result of man's stupidity. They are specifically the "wrath of God."

In verse 2 John sees something that looks like a sea of glass mingled with fire, and on that sea are the saints that have gotten the victory over the beast and the image and the mark. These all have harps. It doesn't sound like this group includes all of the redeemed saints from history, but only those that came out of the great tribulation. I don't know if that is significant or important, but the limited nature of the group is stated clearly. These all have harps and sing the song of Moses and the song of the Lamb. Perhaps those who have endured the greatest persecutions and prevailed will enjoy special attention in heaven. Luke 6:22-23 does suggest that those who suffer persecution and reproach shall receive a "great reward," and the wording implies it is a greater reward than those redeemed of the Lord that do not suffer such persecution.

Now in verse 5 the temple of the tabernacle of the testimony in heaven is opened and the seven angels having the seven last plagues come forth. Each angel, in verse 7, is given a golden vial full of the wrath of God. Verse 8, the temple is filled with the smoke from the glory of God and from his power and it says no man could enter until the plagues were fulfilled. I have no idea the significance of that but keep in mind this is just what John is seeing in the vision and is not a literal description of something happening on earth.

So now, in chapter 16, the angels begin to pour out their vials. The first vial was poured out and a noisome and grievous sore fell upon all those that have the mark of the beast. This is the first indicator as to where this begins on the timeline. Though we may not know precisely when the mark of the beast is given, we do know that these plagues do not begin until after that time. It is encouraging to note that this plague only landed on those who had the mark, or those who worshiped the beast. Thus, the Christians would be separated from this plague much like the Israelites were separated from the plagues of Egypt during the time of Moses.

In verse 3 the second vial is poured out on the sea and it became as the blood of a dead man. Unlike the second trumpet of Revelation 8:8-9, where the sea became blood and only a third of the sea creatures died and a third of the ships were destroyed, this time every living soul in the sea died. Is this referring only to men? Or does it also suggest the animals of the sea, which would suggest that animals have souls? An intriguing question.

Verse 4: The third vial is poured on the rivers and fountains of water which sounds just like the third trumpet of Revelation 8:10. I don't know if these are two different references to the same basic event. During the trumpets it seems only about a third of life was affected by the events while during the vials it seems the devastation is much more complete and widespread. It is interesting to note that while many today would say that such "acts of God" occurring on the earth would suggest that God is a cruel murderous vindictive God, the texts in verses 5 through 7 use words like "true and righteous" to describe him for these acts. The problem is, men fail to perceive themselves as evil while they shed the blood of saints and prophets. The Bible says they are "worthy" of these true and righteous judgments from God.

Verse 8: The fourth angel pours out his vial on the sun and power is given him to scorch men with fire. This starts to parallel with the events referred to earlier in the timeline where the powers of heaven are shaken. Though we know the sun is to go dark because of previous prophecies, here it is suggested that they are scorched with great heat. It is interesting to parallel this passage in verse 9 with Isaiah 30:26 where Isaiah prophesies that in the day that the Lord binds up the breach of his people and heals the stroke of their wound, the light of the moon shall be as the light of the sun, and the light of the sun will be seven fold, as the light of seven days. These events in the sun are very consistent with some sort of nova. The sun first gets very bright. Likely there will be huge radiation storms and coronal mass ejections that will cause burns and great heat on the earth. Shortly after the sun explodes it would then implode into a black dwarf where it would give off very little light. Many novas have been observed in space by astronomers and this is a very normal progression. A nova can take as little as two weeks to complete. As usual, men curse God for these judgments but in arrogance refuse to repent of their deeds.

Now in verse 10 the fifth angel's vial is poured out on the seat of the beast and his kingdom is filled with darkness and they gnawed their tongues for pain. As mentioned in the paragraph above, after the sun goes nova it would implode into a black dwarf which would make it go dark and fill the earth with darkness. Though this may be a spiritual reference to the spiritual darkness of the beast's kingdom, which would also make sense, this could easily be a reference to physical darkness on the earth and fits with other prophecies concerning the sun going dark. The pain men are experiencing is likely the radiation burns caused by the massive energy given off by the sun during the initial expansion phase of the nova. But, again, that is just speculation from the Maybe Box. Nevertheless, something is going to be hurting them. As before, the men of the earth refused to repent of their evil deeds.

With the sixth vial, in verse 12, the great river Euphrates is dried up to make the way for the kings of the East. This would most likely be China but could also be a reference to Iran. In reality, the writings are just not clear on this point.

Verses 13 and 14 are very interesting verses that speak of some unclean spirits "like frogs" that come out of the mouth of the dragon and the beast and the false prophet. Though we know from verse 14 that these are spirits of devils working miracles, I have often wondered if the men of the earth might not believe they are extraterrestrial aliens that look like frogs who have come to warn the world of an impending invasion from another alien force. I have noted an increase of stories in the news media these days about UFO's and aliens suggesting we may soon make contact with extraterrestrials, or at the very least that information is soon to be released verifying the existence of such beings. Are we being psychologically prepared to believe these are really creatures from space with superior intelligence and knowledge of science and that we should listen to them?

Verse 14 says these frogs go to all of the kings of the earth to gather them to a great battle. That battle is referred to as the "great day of God Almighty." No doubt this is a reference to the battle of Armageddon, which is confirmed in verse 16. But before that, in verse 15, Jesus once again warns us to watch and wait for him and to keep ourselves clean and covered that we might not be ashamed at his coming. (1 John 2:28) He reminds us he comes as a thief. This is probably another loose reference to the rapture because the sequence of events described here and in the final verses of this chapter seems to coincide very closely with the sequence of events described in chapter 11:12-13.

Finally, in verse 17, the seventh angel pours out his vial into the air. A great voice comes out of the temple from the throne saying, "It is done." The result is voices, thunders, lightnings and a great earthquake such as was not since men were upon the earth. (v.18) This earthquake matches with the one described in 11:13 which just followed the rapture of the two witnesses, which also most likely occurs at the same time as the general rapture of the saints. This earthquake is so great that it divides the "great city," which is probably a reference to Jerusalem, into three parts and all the cities of the nations fall. Then the great Babylon, which I believe represents the kingdoms of men, comes into remembrance before God (v. 19) and his wrath is poured out. And all hell breaks loose with every island fleeing away (v. 20) and the mountains being made flat. Huge hail stones fall from heaven in a plague described as "exceedingly great." And yet for all of these judgments, men still blasphemed God and refused to repent of their evil deeds. (v. 21)

14. The Whore that Rides the Beast and Babylon is Fallen: Revelation Chapters 17 and 18

Before studying this chapter, read chapters 17 and 18 of Revelation.

Like many other chapters of Revelation, chapters 17 and 18 are highly symbolic. Because of this, it is nearly impossible to know for sure what it all means. Many different speculations have been offered and most interpreters claim to have the riddle solved. Some say the whore is the Catholic Church [CC] and the great false religion of the end times. Others say these chapters are speaking about a literal city of Babylon that, in order to be destroyed, must first be rebuilt. They say this city will be the financial hub used by the man antichrist to control the world financial institutions. Ideas abound. But it is my belief that we will not know for sure what these symbols represent until they begin to come to pass. As is always the case, many previous interpretations of prophecy come about as people attempt to equate the words of prophecy with current world events. That's understandable and, in fact, I do that myself. However, I'm always careful to stipulate my interpretations as speculations that may change as world events and circumstances change. Now, in this chapter, I am going to give you my own speculation as to who the whore represents and what these two chapters are all about. Some things in these chapters obviously connect and relate to things we've already learned about in Daniel and earlier chapters of Revelation. But much here will be speculation. I know this is only a guess, but I include background information to help you see why I have reached this interpretation. You are free, of course, to agree or disagree. But read carefully before you decide.

In chapter 17, one of the angels that had one of the seven vials comes to John and begins to describe to him the judgment of the great whore that sits upon many waters. We will learn many things about this woman but the first point, that she sits upon many waters, says that she sits over or has some impact on many peoples of the world. This is verified by 17:15 where the angel says, "The waters which thou sawest, where the whore sitteth, are peoples, and multitudes, and nations, and tongues." Verse 2 tells us the kings of the earth have committed fornication with her and that the inhabitants of the earth have been made drunk with the wine of her fornication. This is symbolic language and at this point we don't know exactly what he is talking about. But as the story unfolds I believe we will begin to learn that she represents the financial institutions or banking systems of the world. It is with these institutions that all the kings and peoples of the earth have engaged in intercourse, and become drunk with the wealth and power it has generated.

Verse 3: The angel carries John away in the Spirit to a wilderness where he sees a woman sitting on a scarlet colored beast. The beast is full of the names of blasphemy having seven heads and ten horns. This sounds to be the same beast as the one in chapter 13 or the great red dragon of chapter 12 and, no doubt, it does represent the same political system of antichrist. However, we have to keep in mind that this is a different vision and we need to be careful not to project things from the beast of chapter 13 or the dragon of chapter 12 onto the beast of chapter 17 and vice-a-versa. We learn in verse 12 that the ten horns represent the same ten kings as the others but it is unclear at this point what the seven heads represent. At the very least, however, this is the political system of antichrist.

Note that the woman "sits upon" the scarlet colored beast. Generally, when someone is sitting on or riding on a beast, this would suggest they are controlling it like a rider would a horse. It doesn't say that specifically, but the idea is implied. If the whore represents the financial institutions or banking institutions of the world, this would make sense as the ones who pull the purse strings always wield the greatest power and control over the situation. If the whore simply represents the Catholic Church, this would not make sense. For, though the CC at one time in history controlled both the religious power of the world along with the political power of the world, it does so no longer. And it is very unlikely that the CC will regain such spiritual or political power in the future. The CC is not, however, without some financial power in the world, as we shall see further on in this chapter.

Verse 4 begins to describe the whore in more detail. She was arrayed in purple and scarlet color, suggesting royalty and power, decked with gold and precious stones and pearls, suggesting great wealth, having a golden cup in her hand, which we cannot now know for sure what it represents, but it contains the abominations and filthiness of her fornication, which is the result of her financial intercourse with the kings and peoples of the earth. Some would suggest that the golden chalice is symbolic of the Catholic Church, not to mention the colors and the wealth. There may be something to that, but probably not in the way most interpreters think.

In verse 5 it says she had a name written on her forehead, "Mystery Babylon the Great, the Mother of Harlots and Abominations of the Earth." This title troubled me at first. As we work our way through chapters 17 and 18 I believe it will become abundantly clear that this woman represents the financial institutions and monetary system of the world. But I wondered why she was called "Mystery Babylon." I was meditating on this one afternoon lying on my couch when a question popped into my head. "What are the origins of our modern day banking system?" I immediately jumped up to my computer and searched on line for, "Origins of modern day banking system." Guess what popped up: Babylon! The origins of our modern day banking system came from Babylon!

I found several eye opening articles about the origins of our banking system, the Federal Reserve System, the International Monetary Fund and the International Committee of Bankers. One of the things that really surprised me was how the history of our world monetary system is tied in with the Catholic Church. It may be that all of the symbolism of the whore that appears to represent the CC is relevant after all. I did this research a couple of years ago but, unfortunately, I did not print out any of the articles, and now as I sit down to write this book, I find many of those revealing articles have been purged from the internet. I wonder why? I still managed to find some good information and I will reproduce some of it for you here. Unfortunately, I do not have references or web addresses that I can point you to. If you question any of the information below, feel free to begin your own research on the origins of our banking system.

Here are some excerpts from articles I found around September of 2010. Occasionally you will find inserted italicized text enclosed in brackets [*like this.*] These inserts are comments made by me, and do not represent part of the original article.

> The first banks were probably the religious temples of the ancient world, and were probably established in the third millennium B.C. Banks probably predated the invention of money. Deposits initially consisted of grain and later other goods including cattle, agricultural implements, and eventually precious metals such as gold, in the form of easy-to-carry compressed plates. Temples and palaces were the safest places to store gold as they were constantly attended and well built. As sacred places, temples presented an extra deterrent to would-be thieves. There are

extant records of loans from the 18th century BC *in Babylon* that were made by temple priests/monks to merchants.

The Babylonians and their neighbors developed the earliest system of economics that was fixed in a legal code, using a metric of various commodities. The early law codes from Sumer could be considered the first (written) economic formula, and have many attributes still in use in the current price system today, such as codified amounts of money for business deals (interest rates), fines in money for wrongdoing, inheritance rules and laws concerning how private property is to be taxed or divided.

Wealth compressed into the convenient form of gold brings one disadvantage. Unless well hidden or protected, it is easily stolen.

In early civilizations a temple is considered the safest refuge; it is a solid building, constantly attended, with a sacred character which itself may deter thieves. In Egypt and Mesopotamia gold is deposited in temples for safe-keeping. But it lies idle there, while others in the trading community or in government have desperate need of it. In Babylon at the time of Hammurabi, in the 18th century BC, there are records of loans made by the priests of the temple. The concept of banking has arrived.

So now the idea of loaning money from the gold reserves stored in the temple has been discovered. At first the loans were limited to the amount of gold actually stored in the vaults. Loans were made, being covered by other people's money. When the loans were repaid, the temple or "bank" made a profit. They made money from other people's money. But over time they began to realize that they did not need to limit themselves to just the amount of gold that was in the temple. Since there was always some gold in the temple and there was never a time when everyone came at once to get their gold, they began to make multiple loans on the same gold reserve. In other words, they made loans that were not actually backed by sufficient gold in the temple. Again, when the loans were repaid with interest, the "bank" made money. Now they were creating wealth out of "nothing." There are numerous videos on web sites that give a simplified explanation of how our banking system works today. The basic concepts are the same with a few added regulations. A quick web search will yield a wealth of information on the subject.

This article explains how tied in the Catholic Church is to the history and organization of our modern day financial institutions:

Our Modern Banking System Has Roots in History and Religion

The decline of the Roman Empire began in the second century A.D. Once Constantine took the reigns in 306, he took nearly 20 years to restore order within the Empire. Despite the decline, the Empire held much of the wealth of the world at that time. As part an effort to restore order in the Empire, Constantine adopted Christianity as the State Religion, introducing changes by importing customs and cultures into his new religion as a unifying factor for the Roman Empire. The Council of Nicaea formulated the Nicene Creed in 325 and made Christianity the powerhouse of the new Roman Empire as the Roman Catholic Church or World Church. By 476, the political Roman Empire had fallen to repeated outside pressure, transferring the relics of the Roman Empire to the Roman Catholic Church. Political unrest continued as rising powers in Europe invaded the Roman Empire and plundered Rome.

With the rule of the Barbarians and the Byzantines, the Pope became the unquestionable leading religious figure of the time. Local power in Rome was absorbed by the Pope and the remaining possessions of the senatorial aristocracy and the local Byzantine administration in Rome were absorbed by the Roman Catholic Church. The popes of the Church became the de-facto political rulers of Rome and the surrounding regions. Emerging noble families managed to insert a leading role for themselves in the Church. The Popes declared the new Roman Empire through the Roman Catholic Church as the rule of God on earth. Rome was subjected to varying degrees of anarchy and attack until the Normans sacked Rome in 1084. Rome was rebuilt by wealthy families using wealth that came from commerce and banking as the Church began to expand its political and religious power.

Beginning around 1100, the need to transfer large sums of money to finance the Crusades stimulated the current concept of secular banking. The earliest known foreign exchange contract was created in Genoa in 1156. Power struggles by nobles and the Church continued. The Templars and Hospitallers acted as bankers in the Holy Land. Expansive, large land holdings of The Templars across Europe also emerged in the 1100-1300 time frame as the beginning of Europe-wide banking. Their practice was to take in local currency and create a demand note that would be valid at any of their castles across Europe, allowing movement of money without the usual risk of robbery while traveling. Papal bankers were the most successful of the Western world by putting other bankers out of business by force and from trading related to the Crusades.

1300 brought new power and the return of the Popes from France set the stage for a renaissance in Rome. In 1440, the modern printing press established the regular use of paper money. By 1452, the papacy was in firm control of Rome. Rome began to lose its religious character with a great number of popular feasts, horse races, parties, intrigues and licentious episodes as well as an economy rich with the presence of several Tuscan bankers. In 1499, Switzerland acquired its independence from the Holy Roman Empire.

In 1506, Pope Julius II engaged the Swiss Guard that continues to serve the Vatican to the present day. The Sack of Rome in May 1527 marked the end of the initial era of religious-based banking prosperity. Rome had been ransacked and pillaged to point of oblivion by 1540 and Loyola was installed as the point man to stop the demise of Roman Catholic Society. The Bank of Rome was reorganized as a secular organization by Ignacio López de Loyola and the Society of Jesus was founded with commission of reestablishing the stronghold of Rome in the world. Loyola arranged for the Vatican and its holdings to be defended by Swiss mercenaries, commissioned to guard the assets of Rome. Rome decided to store the gold and silver in Switzerland to avoid a repeat of the ransacking of Rome. With this move, the banking system was expanded to the Swiss and from there, an international fraternal body or society of bankers expanded to other locations in the form of "central banking" known today. This history shows the continuing structure and power of the Roman Empire and influence of the Roman Catholic Church in your life today.

The Swiss continue to prosper doing what they have done for years in banking, finance, insurance and protecting the secrets of the wealthy. The Society of Jesus, often referred to as "the Jesuit order", continues to run the day to day operations of the Vatican, the worldwide central banking system and influence multinational financial investment and holding corporations through the Swiss. By this means, the system of central banking is able to sustain and profit through a modern power structure and a global information architecture.

The public stated goals of the Jesuits are concentrated on three activities. They founded universities throughout Europe and the world, which became essential for developing and sustaining the current financial system.

Jesuit teachers are rigorously trained in both classical studies and theology. The Jesuits are to convert non-Christians to Catholicism. Their third goal is to stop Protestantism from spreading and bring the strays back into the religious fold. The leaders of this Society have vowed to bring to pass whatever the papacy demands and have met with great success. The origins of the Roman Empire, Roman Catholic Church and the Jesuit Order are undeniable in the developing history of our current global monetary system while maintaining a current global influence.

Isn't it interesting to see how involved the Catholic Church is in our modern world wide monetary system? This begins to explain, then, the words of Revelation 17:6. "And I saw the woman drunken with the blood of the saints, and with the blood of the martyrs of Jesus…" The persecutions and murderous killings of the true saints by the Catholic Church during the inquisitions which began in the 12th century and continued on into the 16th century easily fulfill the descriptions of this verse. Tying this together with the Catholic Church's deep involvement with the world's financial institutions begins to paint a clear picture.

Here's another article that ties Rome to our Federal reserve system. For this one I have the author's name but not the web site.

The Foundation of the U.S. Federal Reserve by Elvis Manning
This article is copyrighted. Give E. Manning and this website credit.
A summary and early history leading up to the Fed.

Todays central banking system in America is part of a global banking system or Society of Bankers. No less amazing is the fact that the International Society of Bankers has grown as a fraternal brotherhood that functions and supports the secular arm of the Roman Catholic Church, an extension of the old Roman Empire. The move of worldwide assets of the Catholic Church was made originally through the Swiss as they developed a secondary banking system to mimic and enhance the original bank at the Vatican in Rome in a unique partnership of wealth protection. This is a fact that is usually overlooked, conveniently ignored and bathed in other historical details. No less amazing is the fact that this system and the struggle of the International Society of Bankers for prominence and control through this system is responsible for most of the upheaval, war and torment of mankind for the last 2000 years. *[This statement also shows how the whore is responsible for the death and misery of untold millions not related directly to the inquisitions.]* At the core of the matter is the fact that human labor is a very valuable commodity. The controller of that human labor is in charge of everything, for labor is the sum total of everything man does. Therefore, controlling the labor laws and the money regulations along with that is a very important piece of action for the banking system. This is the banking system, imported into the United States in 1913 *[by Woodrow Wilson]* as the Federal Reserve Bank that continues to wield and grow in power over and above the sovereignty of every nation on earth. The illusion of ownership in America today is just that where banking is involved. The Society of Bankers are far too cunning to simply take title to everything they own. You can see how badly the banking system wants to resell foreclosed property. The control isn't about the property, but rather about controlling you and making money on the interest you owe as a debtor. You have been sold the illusion of ownership so that you and your children will continue to work and pay more of your earnings on ever increasing debts that benefit only the Society of Bankers in their rule of the world system! The government and politicians of this country and others have become agents for the Society of Bankers, creating new ways of keeping you in debt to the Society of Bankers. The largest players in Corporate America, like Deloitte Touche, have become as branches of the government, integrally installed within the government as permanent contractors of the United States in function and purpose solely for the purpose of their own profit. To make matters worse, many of these corporate institutions like Deloitte are owned by the Society of Bankers through an institution known as a verein or ownership that is veiled in other ways in a global sense. The Society of Bankers has infiltrated the world accounting houses, the law offices and the management firms of the world, taking all the ownership and profits as they continue to work for the control of the Society of Bankers globally. The Roman Empire is alive and well, working incestuously for the good of itself.

The Bank of Rome was reorganized by Ignacio López de Loyola and the Jesuits were founded with commission of reestablishing the stronghold of Rome in the world after an onslaught of opposition by the nations just before that time. Rome had been ransacked and pillaged to point of oblivion by 1540. Loyola was installed as the point man to stop the demise of Roman Catholic Society and power. The Vatican was and is defended by Swiss mercenaries, commissioned to guard the assets of Rome. Rome decided to store the gold and silver in Switzerland as a precaution to avoid a repeat of the ransacking of Rome. Roman Catholic universities were established to recruit the sharpest minds in order to garner power and strength. The reorganized Bank of Rome began to establish branch offices in various cities. A bank was established in Venice in 1587, Amsterdam in 1609, Hamburg in 1619, Nuremberg in

1621, Rotterdam in 1635 and the Bank of England in 1694. The Bank of England was the first bank to be named after a country after the Bank of Rome, becoming the world's first Central Banking institution after Rome. Since then, many people and governments have fought against the installation of new banks because of the usury exacted by them. England fought the system and lost. The American colonies as well as United States battled the Society of Bankers for hundreds of years until 1913.

~E. Manning

Here is a group of paragraphs taken from an article written by Avro Manhattan. I don't know the date of writing.

A clutch of paragraphs from THE VATICAN BILLIONS by Avro Manhattan:

"The Vatican has large investments with the Rothschilds of Britain, France and America, with the Hambros Bank, with the Credit Suisse in London and Zurich. In the United States it has large investments with the Morgan Bank, the Chase-Manhattan Bank, the First National Bank of New York, the Bankers Trust Company, and others. The Vatican has billions of shares in the most powerful international corporations such as Gulf Oil, Shell, General Motors, Bethlehem Steel, General Electric, International Business Machines, T.W.A., etc. At a conservative estimate, these amount to more than 500 million dollars in the U.S.A. alone.

"In a statement published in connection with a bond prospectus, the Boston archdiocese listed its assets at Six Hundred and Thirty-five Million ($635,891,004), which is 9.9 times its liabilities. This leaves a net worth of Five Hundred and Seventy-one million dollars ($571,704,953). It is not difficult to discover the truly astonishing wealth of the church, once we add the riches of the twenty-eight archdioceses and 122 dioceses of the U.S.A., some of which are even wealthier than that of Boston.

"Some idea of the real estate and other forms of wealth controlled by the Catholic church may be gathered by the remark of a member of the New York Catholic Conference, namely 'that his church probably ranks second only to the United States Government in total annual purchase.' Another statement, made by a nationally syndicated Catholic priest, perhaps is even more telling. 'The Catholic Church,' he said, 'must be the biggest corporation in the United States. We have a branch office in every neighborhood. Our assets and real estate holdings must exceed those of Standard Oil, A.T.&T., and U.S. Steel combined. And our roster of dues-paying members must be second only to the tax rolls of the United States Government.'

"The Catholic church, once all her assets have been put together, is the most formidable stockbroker in the world. The Vatican, independently of each successive pope, has been increasingly orientated towards the U.S. The Wall Street Journal said that the Vatican's financial deals in the U.S. alone were so big that very often it sold or bought gold in lots of a million or more dollars at one time.

"The Vatican's treasure of solid gold has been estimated by the United Nations World Magazine to amount to several billion dollars. A large bulk of this is stored in gold ingots with the U.S. Federal Reserve Bank, while banks in England and Switzerland hold the rest. But this is just a small portion of the wealth of the Vatican, which in the U.S. alone, is greater than that of the five wealthiest giant corporations of the country. When to that is added all the real estate, property, stocks and shares abroad, then the staggering accumulation of the wealth of the Catholic Church becomes so formidable as to defy any rational assessment.

"The Catholic church is the biggest financial power, wealth accumulator and property owner in existence. She is a greater possessor of material riches than any other single institution, corporation, bank, giant trust, government or state of the whole globe. The pope, as the visible ruler of this immense amassment of wealth, is consequently the richest individual of the twentieth century. No one can realistically assess how much he is worth in terms of billions of dollars."

It's all JUST MERGERS & ACQUISITIONS....

Many historians and researchers and one American Congressman stated that : The VATICAN through the Jesuit Order controlling the Illuminatis is in control of the United States Federal Reserve. Whoever controls the Federal Reserve Of New York controls the whole United States Federal Reserve. It was also found out that the Federal Reserve is [not] owned by the government of the United States and in-fact the Federal Reserve is owned by a private entity. GUESS WHO !

Yes, the Catholic Church still wants to rule the world. But this time they are trying to do it through their control of the world's money supply. They are still of the spirit of antichrist.

And finally, here is another article by Manning explaining how our Federal Reserve system works:

by E. Manning

The Federal Reserve Corporation is not a government agency, as people are led to believe. It is a private corporation controlled by the Society of Bankers and run in the limelight by the Vatican through Swiss bankers. This fraternal society of bankers is operated for the financial gain of the Society of Bankers over the people, rather than for the benefit of the people in a particular country or sovereignty outside of the Society of Bankers.

On Christmas Eve in 1913, the U.S. Congress passed the Federal Reserve Act, which officially took the power to create the money to run United States away from the Congress, and gave it over to the Society of Bankers, who called themselves the Federal Reserve Corporation.

The passage of this Federal Reserve Act authorized the establishment of a Federal Reserve Corporation, with a Board of Directors (The Federal Reserve Board) to run it. And the United States was divided into 12 Federal Reserve Districts.

This new law completely removed from the Congress the right to create money or to have any control over its creation, and gave this function over to the Federal Reserve Corporation. The Federal Reserve Bank printed "Federal Reserve Notes", which are still accepted today as money among the citizens of the country.

Because the Congress went against the Constitution of the United States when it passed this Federal Reserve Act Federal Reserve Notes are not actually legal tender, for the constitution specifically states that Congress, and only Congress shall have the power to coin and regulate the money of the country.

The Federal Reserve Notes are accepted as a medium of exchange by the people of the United States. Federal Reserve Notes are a debt-money, with interest charged on every dollar that is created without the interest being created as money.

Let's say the Federal Government needs $5 billion dollars after collecting taxes to continue financing projects. Since the government does not have the money, and Congress has given away its authority to create it, the Government must go to the Federal Reserve, which is in charge of creating the money for the country. The Society of Bankers deliver $5 billion in money or credit to the Federal Government in exchange for the Government's agreement to pay it back with interest! The Congress then authorizes the Treasury Department to print $5 billion in U.S. bonds, which are then delivered to the Federal Reserve Bankers.

The Federal Reserve then pays the cost of printing the $5 billion and makes the exchange. The Government uses the money to pay its obligation. The $5 billion in Government bills is paid, but the Government has now indebted the people to the Society of Bankers for $1 billion, on which the people must pay interest indefinitely unless the debt is paid in real currency! The interest is never created and simply continues to build.

Thousands of transactions have taken place since 1914, so by now the United States Government is indebted to the Bankers for $7,000,000,000,000, ($7 trillion), on which the people pay over $600 billion a year in interest alone, with no hope of ever paying off the principal. Because of the interest charged on the money created, the borrower must always pay back more than he borrowed. Naturally, the Society of Bankers will always get back more than they lend and the debt is never paid in the case of the Government.

There was more, but for the sake of space I'll not insert any more articles. If you want to dive into this any deeper, just do the research on line. But remember, not everything you read can be trusted. I'm not endorsing any of these authors or vouching for the accuracy or truthfulness of their articles. But what I found, as exampled above, certainly bears out in light of Revelation 17 and 18 as we will discuss below.

Continuing with verse 6, at first John marveled at the sight of the woman. But the angel asks him why in verse 7 and begins to explain to him the "mystery" of the woman and the beast that carried her, which had the seven heads and the ten horns.

Verse 8: "The beast that thou sawest was, and is not; and shall ascend out of the bottomless pit, and go into perdition..." The first thing we get from this is that the bottomless pit is not a literal hole in the ground. It seems clear that this is a symbolic representation of something, which has implications for Revelation chapter 9. In chapter 9 of Revelation we saw a lot of stuff from the political system of antichrist coming out of the bottomless pit. One of those things was the "king" over them and was called the angel of the bottomless pit. We know from his names that he is the destroyer but we don't know if this was a reference to the man antichrist or Satan or both. In this case, however, it is a beast, which represents the political system of antichrist and not just the man antichrist. This distinction is important to remember. The whole system and everyone involved with it go into perdition.

But what does he mean by, "…was, and is not…"? I'm not sure. At the end of verse 8 he expands that description as, "…that was, and is not, and yet is." I can go to the Maybe Box and make a guess here, but I don't think anyone can know for sure. There isn't much to go on. Perhaps it is a reference to the kingdoms of men which were of the spirit of antichrist, which ruled the world from the Babylonians through the end of the Roman Empire. After the Romans no kingdom ruled the whole earth. But we know from Daniel that there is a fifth kingdom yet to be seen that is made of iron and clay. Perhaps the 1,600 year gap of no world domination by the political system of antichrist is what is being referred to as, "is not." But under the surface the political aims of antichrist, the desire to rule the world, still bubble, and thus, "and yet is." I don't know. And I'm sure it's not vitally important that we do know.

Verse 9 starts off with, "And here is the mind which hath wisdom." That's a clue to say the following words probably aren't as easy to understand as you might first think. It's going to take some thought and some understanding. The words are, "The seven heads are seven mountains on which the woman sitteth." Ok, here we go. Most scholars accept without question that this is a reference to the city of Rome which is commonly referred to as the City of Seven Hills. And that thought fits in nicely with the Dispensational view that the last kingdom of men on earth will be a revived Roman empire. But that is a huge assumption. You may be surprised to learn that there are no less than 54 cities throughout the world today that are referred to as a City of Seven Hills, not the least of which are Jerusalem and Istanbul, which is Constantinople. Constantinople, the city of Constantine, was the new capital of the Roman Empire when Constantine moved it from Rome around 660 AD. The Roman culture had a huge impact on the Ottoman culture during that time and in that area. The Ottomans are the ancestors of the modern day Muslims. Is this prophetic picture trying to make a connection? Who knows? Maybe the seven mountains are the hills of Istanbul. Istanbul is in Turkey which, today, is another Islamic stronghold and no friend of Israel or Christianity.

But who says these seven mountains represent *any* city? That in itself is an assumption. Maybe it's not a reference to a city at all. There is a world wide Christian movement afoot today called "Reclaiming the Seven Mountains of Culture." I mentioned them earlier. Here's the address of their web site: http://www.7culturalmountains.org. These people are basically of the Dominion Theology persuasion and believe the Church must first rule the world before the Christ can come back. In order to do this Christians must gain power and influence in the seven areas of culture, those being: arts and entertainment, education, family, government, media, religion, and most importantly because it will bankroll all the others, business. I recommend you do some research on this. It is an insidious and dangerous movement among certain Christian circles today. Maybe this is the seven mountains verse 9 is referring to. The reason I say this is because this political movement has the same goal as every other "ism" that is of antichrist. And that goal is to rule the world. I believe this movement within the very bowls of the Christian Church today is actually of antichrist.

The point is, I don't think it's as simple as saying it is Rome. The seven heads are part of the political system of antichrist, not the Catholic Church or Rome. The whore may represent Rome and the Catholic Church's financial control over the beast, but the beast, I believe, is more of a secular representation of the political system of antichrist. It's the political kings and kingdoms of the world that are being controlled by the financial purse strings of the central banking system, which apparently is itself controlled by the Catholic Church. So in summary, I don't know what the seven mountains are and neither does anyone else. The Bible doesn't tell us. But keep your eyes and ears open and when the beast of 10 kings comes to power watch for something that might fit the seven heads as seven mountains.

Verse 10: "And there are seven kings." Most will try to say that these seven kings are also represented by the seven heads. It does not say that. The seven heads are seven mountains. That's the end of that statement. Then the angel goes on to a new subject, "And there are seven kings." The reason I know these are not represented by the seven heads is because in verse 11 we find that this beast with the seven heads is actually the eighth king.

"Five are fallen, and one is, and the other is not yet come; and when he cometh, he must continue a short space." Again, I don't believe it is possible to say with certainty who these kings represent. However, going to the Maybe Box, if we assume the "tenses" of the verbs are relative to John's day, the five that have fallen might be Babylon, the Medes and the Persians, the Greeks, the Seleucids and the Ptolemys, the last two being the two major powers which ruled after the death of Alexander the Great. (I include these because they are prominent kings in the prophecies of Daniel 11; the kings of the North and South.) The one that "is" would be Rome. And the one that is to come would be the final world wide kingdom of men ruled by the 10 kings as described in Daniel. This last king or kingdom with the 10 kings will continue for only a short space before this beast, which is the eighth king, comes to power. Whether or not this is a correct interpretation, I have no idea. It is perhaps a bit of a stretch and doesn't fit perfectly because this last beast also includes the 10 kings. At the very least, however, this last beast, which we must remember represents more than just a man, which is the eighth, is "of the seven" which I believe means he is of the same spirit of antichrist. It seems also clear that this beast represents the last kingdom of man that goes into perdition at the end of all things.

This is born out by verse 12 where the angel says that the ten horns are ten kings. This precisely matches this beast with the beast of Daniel 7:24 where we learned that the 10 horns were 10 kings, which also matched with the 10 toes of the last kingdom of men in Daniel 2. We learned that the 10 kings of Daniel 7 only reigned for a short while before a little horn came up and uprooted three of them. Here in verse 12 of Revelation 17 it says the ten kings have received no kingdom as of yet, which means they are future to the apostle John, but receive power as kings "one hour" with the beast. I don't believe this "one hour" literally means one hour, but rather means a very short period of time. I know that violates my normal rules of literal interpretation, but because of the context and the fact that the other prophecies concerning these ten kings would make no sense if it literally meant one hour, I am comfortable with allowing this wording in this symbolic laden text to mean a short period of time or a few years.

Also note that it says the kings served one hour "with the beast." If the beast represents the man antichrist, this would not make sense because the man antichrist uproots three of the kings when he comes to power and, thus, only rules with the seven remaining. But if the beast represents the political system of antichrist and the last great world kingdom of men then it makes perfect sense with all of the other prophecies that describe this kingdom as beginning with a headship of 10 kings. These 10 kings continue with the beast for a short time before the man antichrist comes on the scene, just as described in Daniel 7. Seven of them continue with the man antichrist until the end.

Now we learn a bit more about these kings in verse 13. "These have one mind…" They are all of the spirit of antichrist. They all want to rule the world and control all of mankind. Maybe they all just want to destroy capitalism, the United States and Israel. But remember, this kingdom is divided being made of iron and clay which won't mix. They will be divided in their loyalties, but in order to bring about the reality of this last world government, "they will give their power and strength unto the beast." They will yield all their power and might to the great political system of antichrist.

Verse 14: "These shall make war with the Lamb and the Lamb shall overcome them." This verse is not trying to give an ordered chronology of events. It is a general reference to the fact that the political system of antichrist, the beast, will make war with God, persecute the saints and seek to destroy them. But in the end, Jesus will overcome him. This is nothing new. We've seen this described many times already in Daniel, the gospels and in earlier chapters of Revelation.

Verse 15: "The waters…are peoples, and multitudes, and nations, and tongues." I said this earlier but it is here confirmed. The whore clearly has great power and influence over many peoples. This fits nicely with the picture of the Catholic Church but also with the power and controlling influence of the international monetary system and the International Committee of Bankers.

Verse 16: Here is a surprise! The ten horns upon the beast, which are the ten kings, they shall *hate* the whore. Whoa! That doesn't seem to make sense. I thought the whore and the beast were of the same spirit and were working together. Now I read that the kings *hate* the whore. Well, when you begin to think about who the whore is, it begins to make more sense. The international monetary system is not controlled by the kings and rulers of the nations. This is a separate world wide system controlled by the International Committee of Bankers. When I originally did my research I found an incredible article describing all kinds of things about this committee. They even had their own web site with an interesting video of an interview with one of the committee members. When I went back to get that information and document it for this book, I could no longer find it. Apparently, they are becoming aware that outside people are looking for this information and they are purging it from the internet.

But here's the thing. The kings of the earth that were made rich and powerful by their fornication with the central banking system are beginning to resent the control it exercises over them. About a year ago I read in the news that President Obama was threatening to sue the Swiss banks if they would not open their records and expose Americans that have hidden funds there, and thus not paid taxes on the money. Going on with verse 16 it says, "…and shall make her desolate and naked, and shall eat her flesh, and burn her with fire." Making her desolate and naked means to remove her covering and expose her secret parts. Isn't that exactly what Obama wants to do with the Swiss banks; expose their secret records? Eating her flesh probably relates to the financial pressures the governments and communist unions of the world are putting on the banks, causing them to fail. Eating them up one bank at a time. Burning her with fire? I don't know what that means, but it certainly sounds fatal to me.

The 10 kings want to collapse the financial systems of the world, retake control of the money, and establish a new world financial order controlled by them and not the banks. Isn't that exactly what we see Obama doing in the United States today? And isn't that exactly what we see happening all around the world? I tell you, I believe the time for this to be fulfilled is just around the corner.

Verse 17: This is all in the plan of God. These kings are unwittingly fulfilling all the will of God by agreeing and giving their power unto the beast. Not one word shall fail Him.

Verse 18: And finally, the angel says that this woman, the whore, the financial institutions and banking systems of the world, are "that great city which reigneth over the kings of the earth." What great city is this referring to? If you want to talk about finances, I think you'd have to say this is referring to New York City. But I don't believe this is referring to a literal city. This is referring to the system of Babylon, the whore, the financial institutions and the centralized banking system of the world. This belief will be verified in Revelation 18:10 when the angel cries out, "Alas, alas that great city Babylon, that mighty city! For in one hour is thy judgment come." Babylon is the mighty city that reigns over the kings of the earth. She is the whore with "Mystery Babylon the Great, the Mother of Harlots and Abominations of the Earth" written across her forehead.

Chapter 18 picks up right where chapter 17 left off. The kings of the earth hate the whore of Babylon and are destroying her. The collapse of the world banks is complete and at last the angel cries out, "Babylon the great is fallen, is fallen, and is become the habitation of devils and the hold of every foul spirit, and a cage of every unclean and hateful bird." What a perfect picture of the putrid men and women that pillaged the world for her wealth and used it to enslave the kings and peoples of the world. But now this system is collapsed completely. Nothing is left of her. The unsustainable world banking system that began in the days of Babylon has finally collapsed of its own weight and excess. The whore is burned up with fire and is gone.

Most of this chapter is self explanatory in light of the understanding that the whore of Babylon is the world monetary system, but I want to just highlight a few of the verses.

Verse 3 says, "…and the merchants of the earth are waxed rich through the abundance of *her* delicacies." The angel is still talking about the whore. The merchants of the earth are made rich by her. If we thought of the whore only as a religious organization, such as the Catholic Church, this doesn't make sense. But as a world monetary system, it does.

Verse 4 is interesting. Another voice comes from heaven and says to the people of God that they should "Come out of her…that ye be not partakers of *her* sins, and that ye receive not of *her* plagues." I think this is a warning to get out of the markets, get out of debt, and as much as possible, get out of the money system. It's all going to collapse. Learn to trust in the Father and live by faith. That will be all you have when the system collapses and you cannot receive the mark of the beast by which to buy or sell.

Verse 7 says, "…for she saith in her heart, I sit a queen, and am no widow, and shall see no sorrow." The owners and rulers of this banking system surely believed that it could never fail. Countries and central banks continued to try to prop up economies while all the time continuing to expand the bubbles and stretch the system. But she was wrong. It all comes down in one day.

Verse 9 is interesting as it says the kings of the earth shall bewail her and lament for her. This must not be talking about the ten kings, or by now the seven kings and the man antichrist, that rule the world because those kings or rulers or principle directors hated the whore. They will be glad it has collapsed. But the rank and file leaders of nations will not be happy because they will have lost all control of the money and economies in their countries to the beast.

Verse 8 says the city, "she," shall be utterly burned with fire, just like 17:16. And 18:9 and 10 says, "…they shall see the smoke of her burning. Standing afar off…" Babylon, that mighty city, for in one hour her judgment is come.

Verses 11 through 17 make it clear that this is all about commerce. Even gold and silver will have no value. Verse 15 says, "…the merchants of these things which were made rich by *her* shall [also] stand afar off for fear of her torment, weeping a wailing."

Verse 17: "For in one hour so great riches is come to nought." Then it goes on to describe how even the ships and all sea going commerce will collapse from this economic disaster.

Verse 20 is interesting. It says, "Rejoice over her, thou heaven, and ye holy apostles and prophets; for God hath avenged you on her." It was she that killed the apostles and prophets and martyred the saints who resisted her. Verse 24 says, "And in her was found the blood of prophets and of saints and of all that were slain upon the earth." Now she is destroyed and they are avenged.

Finally, verse 24 shows that it was not just the deaths of the inquisition that this Catholic Church run world banking system is responsible for. But that she is also responsible for, "…all that were slain upon the earth." Just as the articles quoted above claimed, that these world bankers were responsible for all the wars and unrest in the world for the last 2000 years, so the prophecy says she was the cause of all these deaths. But now…she is gone and a new Kingdom is arriving.

15. *Armageddon and the Millennial Reign of Christ: Revelation Chapters 19 and 20*

For this chapter you should read Revelation, chapters 19 and 20. Also read Ezekiel chapters 38 and 39.

Chapter 19 picks up right where chapter 18 leaves off with the destruction of the great whore creating celebration in heaven. The timeline is not clear in this chapter just as in the last, but the general idea can be gathered from the texts and when seen in the light of the structure from Daniel, a very good guess can be made.

Verses 1 through 6 show a building chorus of celebration at the end of the great whore. It begins in verse 1 with, "…a great voice of much people in heaven…" which gives us the sense that this is after the rapture but before Christ has set foot on the earth. Then it builds until verse 6 where it is described as, "…the voice of a great multitude and as the voice of many waters and as the voice of mighty thunderings…" praising God.

Verse 7 adds a new bit of information to the timeline. Here the angel or the voices said, "Let us be glad and rejoice…for the marriage of the Lamb is come…" Here we see the picture. The whore is defeated, the saints are in heaven, the celebration is ongoing and then it is time for the marriage supper. In verse 8 the bride makes herself ready and in verse 9 it says, "…blessed are they which are called unto the marriage supper of the Lamb." Sometimes people like to confuse these two verses suggesting that the bride is not the same as those invited to the supper. It is an interesting speculation but one that would be hard to confirm in the writings. There are parables in the gospels, such as the one in Matthew 22:2 where the Kingdom of God is compared to a king that made a marriage to his son. The parable speaks of gathering guests to the marriage, but says nothing of the bride. The message of the parable was clear, however, that Jesus was speaking of those that were called to salvation, but preferred not to respond. This was spoken in the presence of and in the context of the Pharisees that rejected him. The parable of the ten virgins also speaks of those entering into the kingdom as the Church who are not referred to in any way as the bride. But we are also referred to as the Bride in John 3:29. So there is precedence for speaking of the Church of Jesus Christ as guests at a wedding as well as speaking of them as the Bride of Christ. I don't believe there is any scriptural reason to try to distinguish one from the other or to say that the Bride is a select group of elite Christians while the guests are the common rank and file. In fact, as we get into chapter 21 of Revelation we will find a symbolic picture of the Bride of Christ that includes not only all the saints of the New Testament, but also those from the twelve tribes of Israel.

Now in verse 11, following the marriage ceremony, we see Jesus coming in on his white horse. This is the representation of his grand entrance onto the earth. Verse 14 says he is followed by "his armies" on white horses. Does this include all of the saints or is it just the 144,000 we learned about in chapter 14? It doesn't say. Perhaps we will ride in with him on that great day. That would be glorious. It does say in verse 14 that these armies are, "...clothed in fine linen, white and clean..." just as the bride was arrayed in verse 8. And there is a verse in Zechariah 14:5 that suggests when the Lord comes he will come with "....all his saints." Perhaps we will all be included in that glorious event. But what we know for sure is, this is the beginning of the final wrath of God, the day of our Lord's judgment.

Verses 17 and 18 are the cry of the angel announcing that there is soon to be a great battle with many deaths. The angel is calling for carrion eating fowls to gather and prepare to feast on the flesh of kings, and of captains, and of mighty men and their horses. The stage is being set for the great battle of Armageddon as we saw in Revelation 16:16. Joel 3:14 describes it as, "Multitudes, multitudes in the valley of decision, for the day of the Lord is near in the valley of decision." In Joel 3:2 it is described as, "the valley of Jehoshaphat."

Now, Ezekiel 38 and 39 also speak of a great epic battle between Israel and "Gog of the land of Magog" who was the, "chief prince of Meshach and Tubal." Many scholars like to suggest that this battle is a different war from Armageddon that must be fought with Israel before the beginning of the seven year tribulation period, but there are problems with that view.

Ezekiel 38:8 speaks of this battle taking place, "in the latter years" in a "land that is brought back from the sword." It is speaking of Israel and says, "...they shall dwell safely all of them." Though Israel has definitely become the land brought back from the sword when they were re-established in 1948, I don't think it would be accurate to say that Israel has dwelled "safely" anytime since. They are under constant attack and threat of attack from the Syrians, Palestinians, Iranians and now even Egypt. This term "in the latter years" is more likely a reference to the first half of the 70th week of Daniel when Israel is again establishing their covenant and everyone is saying, "peace and safety" (but then sudden destruction is upon them. I Thess. 5:2-3). This idea of peace and safety is repeated in verses 38:11 and 38:14. But Ezekiel 38:5 and 6 list Persia (Iran), Ethiopia, Libya and "many people with thee" that will come upon Israel suddenly. 38:9 says Gog will ascend like a storm and come upon Israel, "...and many people with thee." This is again repeated in verse 15. So, many nations of the world will be involved in this war, just as it will be in Armageddon. And before it can start, Israel must be in a time when they are saying "peace and safety." Currently, they are not.

Ezekiel 38:16 makes a very clear statement, "It shall be in the latter days." Now some like to say the whole two thousand years since Christ are the "latter days." I don't buy it. I believe when I hear the term "latter days" in prophecy it is speaking, at most, of the last 7 years but more likely only of the last three and a half years before and during His actual return.

In 38:16 God also says that from this battle, "the heathen may know me, when I shall be sanctified in thee." Couple this with 38:23 which says, "Thus will I magnify myself, and sanctify myself; and I will be known in the eyes of many nations, and they shall know that I am the LORD." Then 39:21, "And I will set my glory among the heathen, and all the heathen shall see my judgment that I have executed, and my hand that I have laid upon them." And again in 39:23, "And the heathen shall know..." All of these verses and more suggest that the nations of the heathen that come against Israel will know that it was the hand of the Lord that delivered Israel. If this is so, and this battle precedes the 70th week of Daniel, how is it that all of these nations so quickly forget this deliverance and begin once again to gather themselves against Israel when they finally do get into the 70th week? Another hint is Ezekiel 39:9. This verse says that after this battle the Israelites will burn the weapons of their enemies for seven years. If that's true then the beginning of the 70th week has to be many years down the road from the end of this battle. So, either this separate war occurs many, many years before the end times so that the thrashing by God is forgotten, or this is not a separate war, but rather a description of all the battles that will be fought in Israel from the abomination of desolation unto the great battle of Armageddon.

Ezekiel 38:17 is another verse that must be explained if this battle is a separate battle from Armageddon. In verse 17 God says through the prophet that, "Art thou he of whom I have spoken in old time by my servants the prophets of Israel, which prophesied in those days many years that I would bring thee against them?" He also says this in 39:8, "…this is the day whereof I have spoken." There are no other scriptures in the prophets that speak of any other great battle such as is described in these two chapters except those prophecies that speak of the great battle of Armageddon at the day of the Lord. If this battle, spoken of in Ezekiel 38 and 39, is a prophecy of a separate and distinct war to occur before the beginning of the 70th week, the prophecy stands alone in the words of the prophets. Nowhere else do you find this battle mentioned. But if this is the last great battle that is being prophesied here, then these words of verse 38:17 and 39:8 are true. For that last great battle has been prophesied many times by the prophets.

Ezekiel 38:19-20 speaks of a "great shaking in the land of Israel." We saw this described in Revelation 11:13 and 16:18-19. Notice how in 38:20 he says, "…shall shake *at my presence*, and the mountains shall be thrown down, and the steep places shall fall…" When Jesus comes is when these things will happen. Look at Nahum 1:5 and Amos 9:13. Also Zechariah 14:3-4. Ezekiel 38:22 and the "great hailstones" also remind me of Revelation 16:21. The similarities are striking.

Ezekiel 39:6 speaks of God sending fire upon Magog. This is consistent with almost every other prophecy that speaks of the battle at the Return of Christ. (See Nahum 1:5) They consistently speak of fire.

It is also interesting to note that these three names, Magog, Meshach and Tubal were all children of Japheth, the son of Noah. Therefore, they represent people groups. Experts who claim to know the migration patterns of people groups from Noah's time (an incredible claim in my view) like to say this speaks directly of Russia. Maybe, but maybe not. More likely it represents all Caucasian peoples including those that migrated to the United States. So I don't think we can know for certain who this is referring to, nor does it matter.

Also, note the similarity of wording between Revelation 19:17, 18 and that of Ezekiel 39:4 and 39:17-20. In both cases the writings use very similar texts to describe the gathering of the vultures and the *type* of meat they will be feasting on.

For all of these reasons, I am convinced that this battle is indeed just another perspective on the continual war that will rage from the time of the abomination of desolation unto the great battle of Armageddon and not a separate battle that must be fought a decade or more prior to the seven year period.

Returning to Revelation 19 and verse 19, here is the great gathering of the armies of the beast. In this narrative and the verses that follow, little time is spent describing the battle. The beast and the false prophet are both cast alive into the lake of fire. And all the rest were slain by the word of Christ, which is the sword that comes from his mouth, fulfilling his prophecy in John 12:48. And, just as in Ezekiel 38 and 39, all the fowls were filled with their flesh.

Chapter 20 carries on without pause. Satan, seen in the vision in the form of a dragon, is chained and cast into the bottomless pit. Verse 2 says he is bound, however, only for a thousand years, after which he is loosed a little season. So now we begin to see the timeline extended. We have the judgment of the whore, the celebration in heaven, the wedding of the Lamb, the return of Christ to the earth, the battle of Armageddon, the utter destruction of the beast and the false prophet and finally the binding and imprisonment of Satan himself for a thousand years. This is most likely followed by the judgment seat of Christ where he separates the sheep from the goats. So now Christ is returned to the earth. But there is yet a thousand more years of history to be lived.

Now in chapter 20, verse 5, John sees thrones and those that sat upon them and judgment was given to them. This is the fulfillment of the words of Paul in I Corinthians 6:2-3, "Do ye not know that the saints shall judge the world? … Know ye not that we shall judge angels?"

Back to verse 5, and he saw those that were, "…beheaded for the witness of Jesus and for the word of God and which had not worshipped the beast…." Beheaded? This is new. This little hint of what will be happening during this great persecution is another indicator to me that the face of the man antichrist is much more likely to be Muslim than European. In the Islamic religion, if you refuse to convert to their beliefs you are beheaded. No ifs, ands or buts about it. This is already happening today. I also couple this thought with the fact that when the man antichrist comes to power the first place he goes after is Jerusalem. Shades of the crusades. It is only the Islamic Muslims that are interested in Jerusalem. No other bidder for world domination cares that much about the city. I believe the man antichrist will be Muslim, not European.

Then this statement, "…and they lived and reigned with Christ a thousand years." There are many and varied arguments about the millennium. Some say it is long past, others say it is only a spiritual reference and not literal and others say other crazy things. I don't know all of the different arguments and, frankly, I don't care. I can't see how the writings could be any plainer than this. It states specifically in verses 2, 3, 4, 5, 6 and 7 that there is a thousand year period that follows the return of Christ to earth. Yet still there are those that deny it.

Verse 4 says the resurrected and glorified saints will live and reign with Christ a thousand years. This agrees with the statements made in Daniel 7:18. Verse 5 says, "this is the first resurrection" for the rest of the dead do not live again until the thousand years are finished. This thought is repeated in verse 6. "Blessed and holy is he that hath part in the first resurrection. On such the second death hath no power." What is the second death? That is described in verse 14, the Lake of Fire. The first death is simply the separation of the soul from the body. But the second death is the separation of the soul from God. Once in the Lake of Fire, there is no rescue. For the Lake of Fire, I believe, is a place where God is not.

But jumping back to verse 7, it says that after the thousand years are over Satan will be let loose again and will go out to "Gog and Magog" to once again attempt to do battle with Jesus. It just seems that Lucifer never gets the message. He can't win. But it also just goes to show that mortal man also never seems to get the message. Even after a thousand years of peace on the earth by the rule of Christ, they are still easily deceived into rebelling against him. And Satan rouses up an army to surround Jerusalem, the camp of the saints. God simply sends down fire from heaven and devours them. This time, however, Satan, who is the devil, is

174

cast into the Lake of Fire where the beast and the false prophet are, and there they shall be tormented forever and ever.

Now verse 11 says that after the thousand years are complete, there is a "Great White Throne" judgment. It says everyone in heaven and earth fled away from the face of God on this throne, but they could find no place to hide. You cannot hide from the face of God. And as the text continues the books are opened and everyone who was not written in the Book of Life was judged by their works that were written in the other book. And since all have sinned, none who are not covered by the cross and the blood of Christ will be found worthy to enter into heaven.

In verse 14 we find "death and hell" cast into the Lake of Fire. This can be confusing for some. Actually, the Lake of Fire is "hell" as we know it. The word translated "hell" in this verse is actually the word, "hades," which I understand to be a temporary place of holding for the unrighteous dead. Since all are now judged, there is no longer a need for such a place. And since all living are now either redeemed or judged, there is no need for death. Both are disposed of forever, along with all those whose names were not written in the Book of Life.

It would seem this marks the end of the story. But in truth, there is one more step in the timeline. Chapter 21, verse 1, should have been included at the end of chapter 20 because it goes with chapter 20. The end of the story of chapter 20 is that after all things that offend are cast into the Lake of Fire, John sees a new heaven and a new earth, for the first heaven and first earth are passed away. And apparently, on this new earth, there will be no more sea. In our next chapter we get just a glimpse of this new world.

16. The New Jerusalem and The Bride of Christ: Revelation Chapters 21 and 22

For this chapter, read chapters 21 and 22 of Revelation.

Chapter 21 really begins with verse 2 where John sees the *New* Jerusalem coming down from God out of heaven. This new city is prepared *like* a bride adorned for her husband. We have to be very careful how we parse these words. There is a lot of discussion about whether or not this city, which is decorated and dressed up *as if it were* a bride, is the same thing John sees starting in verse 9. I'll discuss this more when I get to verse 9. But for now, let me just point out that this text *does not say* that this New Jerusalem *is* the bride. It's just prepared *like* a bride. I also want to note that it says this new city is, "coming down from God out of heaven." There is no explanation in the text for this wording and any guess on the matter would be pure speculation. But for now I would just say, it probably means exactly what it says.

Verse 3 is significant. In Zechariah 14 starting in verse 16 and on to the end of the book, Zechariah says that during the millennial reign of Christ all nations shall go up year by year to Jerusalem to celebrate and commemorate the Feast of Tabernacles. The Feast of Tabernacles occurs on the 15th day of the 7th month, fifteen days after the Feast of Trumpets. Though the writings do not say it specifically, it seems clear that the Feast of Tabernacles is to celebrate and commemorate the fact that Jesus our King now "tabernacles" among us. Revelation 21:3 seems to reinforce this idea with, "…the tabernacle of God is with men…" However, this text seems to come in our timeline *after* the thousand year reign and during the new heavens and the new earth. So I wouldn't want to make too much of it.

The reason I believe this New Jerusalem is a reference to a city that exists after the millennial reign and during the new heavens and new earth is because of verse 4. In verse 4 it says, "…there shall be no more death…" During the millennial reign of Christ, there will still be mortals on the earth. Prophecy makes this pretty obvious. Therefore, there will still be death. But once death is cast into the Lake of Fire, there shall be no more mortals, for there shall be no more death. Thus, this has to be speaking of a city during the time of the new heavens and the new earth. Verse 5 reinforces this by saying, "Behold, I make all things new."

Now verses 6 through 8 seem to jump out of the current picture and returns to the realities of where things are with John and with us. God wants us to know these things: 1. "I will give to him that is athirst of the fountain of the water of life freely." 2. "He that overcometh shall inherit all things; and I will be his God, and he shall be my son." 3. "The fearful and unbelieving and the abominable and murderers, and whoremongers, and sorcerers, and idolaters, *and all liars,* shall have their part in the lake which burneth with fire and brimstone: which is the second death." Important words of advice to heed.

Verse 9 begins a whole new vision. One of the seven angels with the vials comes to John and says to him, "I will show thee the bride, the Lamb's wife." Now this is not a city adorned *like* a bride. This time it *is* the bride. However, we know that the bride of Christ is not a city made with brick and mortar or any other earthly substance. Rather, it is made up of the saints of God, who are glorified people. Therefore, we know from the get-go here, that what we are about to hear is a *symbolic representation* of the bride of Christ. Just like the beasts with seven heads and ten horns of earlier chapters represented a political system of antichrist, *in reality made up of people*, and just like the Great City of Babylon, which was the whore, was a symbolic picture of the world monetary system, *in reality made up of people*, so this picture of the bride of Christ, presented as a great and glorious city, is a symbolic representation or picture of the multitudes of people that make up the redeemed bride of Christ.

Now many dispute this idea because of the words in verse 10. John is carried away in the spirit and is shown, "...that great city, the holy Jerusalem, *descending out of heaven from God."* Those words are similar to what he said back up in verse 2 when the New Jerusalem was, "...coming down from God out of heaven." But even though those words are similar, the pictures are not the same. Verse 2 is not couched in symbolic language and is a description of a *city* adorned like a *bride.* In verse 10 the angel is beginning a long symbolic description of a vision that shows a *bride* that looks like a *city.* There is a distinct difference.

In the verses that follow a very detailed description is given of a huge, beautiful and brightly lit city adorned with jewels and gold. A more wonderful sight one could not behold. What do all of these things represent? I don't know. And no one else does either. But we can glean some interesting facts about the bride of Christ if we look at these verses carefully.

For example, there is much debate these days among some Christian circles, as to who the bride of Christ actually includes. As I mentioned earlier, some believe that only a select few, perhaps of the end times saints, actually make up the bride and the rest are just guests at the ceremony. There is also some disagreement as to whether or not the saints before the cross of Christ, those of Israel of old that are saved through faith, are a part of the bride. Is it just the Church or does it include all the redeemed?

Well, our first clue lies in verse 12. This verse tells us there are twelve gates. And the names written on the gates are the names of the twelve tribes of the children of Israel. I would say this conclusively means that all the redeemed of Israel, even those before the Cross of Christ, are a part of the bride of Christ. Then verse 14 tells us there are twelve foundations. The names here are the names of the twelve apostles. This tells me that the bride of Christ includes at least the earliest saints of the Church, the apostles. Whatever else gates and foundations may mean, I'm of the opinion that the bride of Christ includes all the redeemed of the world throughout all the history of the world.

The next clue that this is a symbolic representation and not a literal brick and mortar city is verse 22 where it says, "And I saw no temple therein: for the Lord God Almighty and the Lamb are the temple of it." Ok, God and Jesus are not going to become a brick and mortar temple. This is symbolic. Verse 23 says, "And the city had no need of the sun...for...the Lamb is the light thereof." Jesus is not a literal light. This is spiritual symbolism.

Verse 24 also gives us an interesting insight to the bride of Christ. Remember, the wedding took place just before Jesus set foot on the earth, the battle of Armageddon, and the establishing of His throne on the earth. Verse 24 places us back into the millennium by saying, "And the nations [mortals] of them which are saved shall walk in the light of it: and the kings of the earth [mortals] do bring their glory and honour into it." There will be mortals interacting with the bride of Christ which places her in the millennium.

Chapter 22 continues with the wonderful description of the bride of Christ and gives us more hints about what things are going to be like during the reign of Christ. Once again, in verse 2 we see evidence that this is during the millennial reign when it says, "…and the leaves of the tree were for the healing of the nations." If there were no nations or peoples in need of healing, this would not make any sense.

In verse 5 we see that there is no day or night and no need for a candle or the sun, for the Lord God gives them light. Well, it's a good thing because we learned earlier that the sun is going to go dark. Things on earth will be quite different during the millennial reign.

And finally, in verses 14 and 15 we see this, "Blessed are they that do his commandments, that they may have right to the tree of life, and may enter in through the gates into the city, for without are dogs, and sorcerers, and whoremongers, and murders, and idolaters, and whosoever loveth and maketh a lie." In the new heavens and the new earth, there will be no such beings anywhere. But during the millennial reign of Christ, there will still be mortals. And even though they survived the purging of Christ's fire at his return, they will still be men with sin natures; men who need Christ as their savior.

The rest of the verses of chapter 22 are just closing up the book with a warning to those that would attempt to add to or take from the words of this book. The consequences are dire. For that reason, it behooves anyone, including myself, who would be so brave as to attempt to explain the words of this book to be very careful not to reach conclusions, or to teach conclusions that cannot be easily seen from these texts. It is one thing to speculate and to talk about possible meanings and interpretations where things are vague. It is quite another to take those guesses and speculations and teach them as undisputed truth. In my mind this amounts to "adding to this book." And I have no desire to join those ranks.

17. Closing Remarks

Most of what I have written in this book has come from clearly stated facts found in the writings of the Bible, but much of what I have said is merely my opinion or speculation. I have tried very hard to be careful to distinguish between the two. Facts are facts and don't change. But speculations must always be held loosely. I have read and re-read this book trying to discover and edit any speculations that were not labeled as such. If I missed any, I hope you will be forgiving and gracious. At the same time, I hope you have been made more aware of the clear facts of prophecy, and been enabled to see the unquestionable framework and timeline of the latter day events. With this framework securely in mind you will now not only be better equipped to recognize the important prophetic events when they occur, but you will also begin to discover other Bible prophecies and texts in the writings that reinforce and flow easily with it. As you read through the gospels, the epistles, the prophets and the Psalms, you will time and time again find yourself saying, "I can see where that fits now." And hopefully you will begin to discover the consistency and congruence of the all the prophecies of the Bible; especially as it relates to those things that occur In the Latter Days.

May the Lord God Almighty be with you as you continue your search for truth.

Addendum: The Rapture of the Church. When will it be?

I've covered this topic pretty thoroughly in earlier chapters but to help you put it all together I have gathered here into one place all of the scriptures that relate or even seem to relate to the rapture of the Church. This addendum will also include references from the epistles which we have not previously covered. Hopefully, this will help to dispel any questions you have concerning this "controversy."

First, the obvious ones.

Matthew 24:31

In Matthew 24, Jesus is answering the question from his disciples, "…what shall be the sign of thy coming and of the end of the world?" (Matt. 24:3) Jesus gives a detailed description of events which, without the structure of Daniel's timeline, might be difficult to understand in chronological order. But by the time he gets to verse 30 he is clearly at the end of his chronology for he says, "…they shall see the son of man coming *in the clouds* of heaven with power…" Immediately *after* that (verse 31) he sends his angels *with the great sound of a trumpet* and gathers *his elect* from the four winds of heaven, from one end to the other. This is the rapture and that is the end of his chronological narrative.

The references to Jesus' return "in the clouds" are numerous. Almost every reference to his return includes them. This is as he returns *to the earth*. There are *no references* that say he will come part way down to get the saints and then go away again for seven years before returning finally to set foot on the earth. None! He comes once when he comes. And he will come in a cloud. And we will go to meet him in that cloud.

It is interesting to note that Jesus made *no mention* of any kind of gathering of saints early on in his description of the last days. The only such gathering mentioned occurred *at the end*. This is significant.

It occurs *with the great sound of a trumpet*. This is also significant and must be remembered.

Mark 13:27

Mark's version of this same narrative by Jesus is very similar to Matthew's. In Mark 13:26 he says, "And then shall they see the Son of man coming *in the clouds* with great power and glory." Verse 27 says, "And then shall he send his angels, and shall gather together his elect from the four winds, from the *uttermost part of the earth* to the uttermost part of the heavens."

Once again, this gathering occurred at the end of Jesus' narrative and again it *followed* the seeing of Jesus coming *in the clouds.* In Matthew it was stated that the saints were gathered from one end of *heaven* to the other. But if there was any question as to whether or not this included the elect still on the earth, Mark puts that to rest by stating they also came from the uttermost parts *of the earth.*

Again, there was no mention in Mark of any other kind of gathering or rapture that was to occur at an earlier time in the chronology of end time events. If such an event were in the plan, you'd think it would be significant enough to be mentioned by Jesus. But there is no such mention.

Now, let's go to the epistles.

I Thessalonians 4:16-17

"For the Lord himself *shall descend from heaven* with a shout, with the voice of the archangel, *and with the trump of God,* and the *dead in Christ shall rise* first. Then we which are alive and remain *shall be caught up together* with them *in the clouds* to meet the Lord in the air…"

Just as in Matthew and Mark, the Lord shall be coming (descending). At that time there will be the *trumpet blast* of God. We will meet with him *in the clouds.* And it is also significant to note that we are caught up together *with the resurrected saints* that have already died. The resurrection occurs at the same time as the rapture.

So, apparently, Paul also places the rapture at the same time that Jesus did. But there is more.

"Behold, I show you a mystery. We shall not all sleep but we shall be changed, in a moment, in the twinkling of an eye, *at the last trump*, for the trumpet shall sound, and the *dead shall be raised* incorruptible, and *we shall be changed*."

Though these verses do not blatantly state the rapture, it is clearly implied. And this is further verified by making the event coincidental with *the trump of God* and the resurrection from the dead. But this is not just *the* trump of God, this is *the last* trump of God. We know from Matthew 24:31 and 1 Thess. 4:16 that a trumpet sounds when Jesus returns. If this isn't *the last trump*, then the resurrection and *change* that Paul speaks of here would have to occur sometime later still. But I think it is clear that this is a reference to the same trump of God that sounds at Jesus' return.

Let's jump back now for a moment to Daniel 12:1-2. As discussed in earlier chapters, this verse appears to speak of a "deliverance" of people which may or may not be a reference to a rapture. In particular, it is not clear as to exactly where in the timeline this event is to occur. But what it does clearly do is to tie this "deliverance" to a resurrection of the dead. The deliverance of the living occurs at the same time as the resurrection from the dead. This agrees with Paul's description above of the rapture occurring simultaneously with the resurrection of the dead.

Now let's look at some other verses that are not as specific but clearly agree with the rapture being at the end of the tribulation when Christ returns.

1 Corinthians 15:23. "But every man in his own order: Christ the firstfruits; afterword they that are Christ's *at his coming.*" We shall be "made alive" (v. 22) at his coming.

John 6:39, 40, 44, 54 Four times in John 6 Jesus says, "...and I will raise him up *at the last day.*" This is more a reference to the resurrection than the rapture, but we've already established that these two events occur at the same time. They will occur at the last day. And don't try to soften this to mean the last *days* or to refer to a larger period of time. When Jesus said the last *day* he meant the last *day*. The "last day" does not come seven years before the last day.

Matthew 24:40-42

We discussed verses 40-42 earlier. This is not a clear reference to the rapture, but does speak of people being "taken" and in context could easily be a reference to this event. In either case, verse 42 makes it pretty clear that this occurs at the hour the Lord comes. Not seven years earlier.

Matthew 25:10

The parable of the 10 virgins. Again we discussed this earlier. The language is symbolic but at the very least we can assume the 10 virgins represent the Church, part of which is wise and part foolish. Without trying to explain the whole parable again, the key point for us here is found in verse 10. "…they that were ready went in with him to the marriage…" When did that happen? "…while they went to buy, *the bridegroom came…*" They went in when he came.

Luke 21:27-28

Luke 21 is Luke's rendition of the same narrative of Jesus that we saw in Matthew 24 and Mark 13. The reason I left it to here is because Luke does not specifically mention the rapture or the gathering of the elect. But in verse 27 we find ourselves at the same point in the timeline with, "And then shall they see the Son of man coming *in a cloud* with power and great glory." Though Luke doesn't mention the gathering at this point, what he does say is, "…look up and lift up your heads; for your redemption draweth nigh." Clearly the elect are still on earth at this point, and also clearly, their redemption is just about to follow his coming at the end of the tribulation.

1 John 2:28 is another reference that does not specifically mention the rapture, but places us at the time of his coming. "And now, little children, abide in him; that, *when he shall appear* we may have confidence, and not be ashamed before him *at his coming."*

In Revelation 7:9 John suddenly sees, "…a great multitude, which no man could number, of all nations, and kindreds, and people, and tongues, stood before the throne…clothed with white robes…" We discussed this before. Though this is not an obvious reference to the rapture, it is interesting that as we follow the timeline of events through chapters 6 and 7 of Revelation and the opening of the seals, the point at which this sudden gathering of saints occurs is right before the seventh seal (Rev. 8:1) which represents, at least, the end of the tribulation period and the beginning of Christ's reign. So, it fits with all the other prophecies and texts concerning the rapture that place it at the end of the tribulation period just prior to the physical return of Jesus to the earth.

Rev. 11:11-12

In Revelation 11, we have the story of the two witnesses. As we discussed earlier, these two men accomplish their ministry during the final three and a half years of the tribulation. In Revelation 11:11-12 is the description of *their* rapture. It is a very clear description of their first being resurrected to life, then being called by a great voice in heaven to "come up hither." Note in verse 12 that it says, "And they ascended up to heaven *in a cloud.*" Sound familiar? Note also that this event occurs at the same time as all of the other resurrection and rapture prophecies, at the end of the tribulation period, just prior to Christ setting foot on the earth.

Revelation 12:1-2

This is a very loose connection, but I don't think it insignificant that this reference to the first day of the seventh month, marked by the sun being in the body of Virgo which is the representation of a woman, and the moon at her feet, was included here in the narrative. As discussed earlier, the first day of the seventh month is the Feast of Trumpets. It is commonly believed (including by me) that this feast is associated with the rapture and/or the return of Christ. Whether it is or not, I think it interesting and significant that this feast is called the Feast of *Trumpets* and that it is prophetically highlighted here in the text of Revelation. This ties it together with the other more obvious references of the trump of God or the last trump occurring at Christ's return and the rapture.

(Update 2017: See chapter 10 of this book for some recently updated information about Revelation 12:1 and this woman in the stars.)

And lastly, this verse in Revelation 14:14 depicts a symbolic picture of the Son of Man, who is Christ, *sitting on a cloud*, who thrust in his sickle and reaped the earth. Again, this is only a loose tie to the rapture, but once again we have the picture of Jesus the Christ coming *in a cloud* and reaping his saints from the earth. The symbolic representation once again places it at the end, as he comes, and just prior to the battle of Armageddon (vs. 18-20) which Jesus himself will preside over when he places is feet on the Mount of Olives (Zechariah 14:4).

There are *no other* scriptures that refer to the rapture that I can find. If they are there, they are so remote and vague as to be highly questionable. But this discussion would not be complete without mentioning the vague and questionable texts used by the Dispensationalists to justify or verify their claim to a "pre-tribulation" rapture. You can not start with the references and use them to build the picture because that simply does not work. And apparently this is not the method of interpretation used by the Dispensationalist. Rather, you must first start with the conclusions and then attempt to justify them or verify them using the Bible.

The assumption that the rapture must occur before the beginning of the last seven year period is based on the concept of "Dispensationalism" which was *invented* for the most part by a man named John Darby in 1830. (Update 2017: I have since learned that the concept of Dispensationalism and the "secret rapture" was the invention of Ignatius Loyola, the founder of the Jesuit order of the Catholic Church, in the mid 1500's. It was an attempt by the Pope to counter the teachings of a post tribulation rapture which was believed by the early fathers of the Protestant reformation. So Darby likely got the idea from him.) Later in the 1800's Dispensationalism was picked up and spread by Dwight L. Moody. In the early 1900's it was made widely popular in the United States by Cyrus Scofield and the publication of the Scofield Reference Bible. Lewis Sperry Chafer was heavily influenced by Scofield and in 1924 founded the Dallas Theological Seminary which has become the flagship of Dispensationalism in America. Now Dispensationalism is everywhere and widely accepted in the vast majority of Christian Churches in the United States.

In a nut shell, Dispensationalism is the belief that God interacts with man differently during different dispensations using different covenant agreements. There is disagreement, however, on how many dispensations there are. Some say there are as many as eight. Others say there are only three. The main point for us to get from this is that the dispensationalist believes that the way God interacts with man or relates to man during the "church age" or "age of grace" is not the same as the way he related to man during the "dispensation of law," which would be the period of the Levitical Law of Moses. Nor will it be the same during the "tribulation" or seven year period. During the tribulation the dispensationalist believes God's rules for interaction with man will change or revert back to something like what they were during the "dispensation of law." The "dispensation of grace" or the "church age" will have necessarily ended at the beginning of the tribulation and God's way of salvation will be different than it is now. In order for Dispensationalism to be true, the Church *must* be taken out when the dispensation of grace, or the "Church" age ends. If it is not, then Dispensationalism *breaks down as a valid theology.*

So, with this *conclusion* already firmly established, the search for proof or verification of this theory begins. Here are the verses I am aware of that relate specifically to the rapture. The theology is very elaborate, complicated and nuanced so I may have missed some. But I believe these examples are the primary foundations of their thinking on this subject.

Luke 21:36 "Watch ye therefore and pray always, that ye may be accounted worthy to escape all these things that shall come to pass..."

Rev. 3:10 "Because thou hast kept the word of my patience, I also will keep thee from the hour of temptation, which shall come upon all the world, to try them that dwell upon the earth."

As discussed earlier in the book, these two verses are often quoted to show that the church will be "accounted worthy to escape" or that Jesus will "keep thee from the hour of temptation" which shall come. Well that sounds good, but there is *nothing* in these texts that suggest this will be done by rapture. There are many ways that the Father could provide for us escape. In fact, as discussed earlier in the book, there will clearly be a group, referred to in Revelation 12:6 and 12:14 as the woman (Israel), that will be carried away somewhere and preserved for the last three and a half years as the antichrist persecutes the Jews and the saints. More likely this is what Jesus was referring to in Luke 21:36 and Revelation 3:10. There are other verses that appear to link to this same idea. They are only loosely related and it would be difficult to show that they definitely are speaking of this group that is hidden away, but I include them here for completeness. They are Zephaniah 2:3, Isaiah 33:15-16, and Isaiah 26:20-21.

Isaiah 57:1 offers insight into another possible way a saint might escape the difficult things that are to come upon the earth during this time. This is confirmed by Revelation 14:13. We might not think of death as the best way out, but knowing that as a believer in Christ we never really die, God will undoubtedly use this method of escape on many of his worthy saints that will be martyred for Christ.

1 Thess. 5:9 "For God hath not appointed us to wrath, but to obtain salvation by our Lord Jesus Christ..."

Though this verse says absolutely nothing about the rapture, I have heard it referenced as proof that the Church will not be on earth during the tribulation. The logic is, the tribulation is the time of God's wrath and since we are not appointed unto wrath we can not be here. That doesn't quite do it for me. Though the Church will be under heavy persecution and will be being purified and made white as Daniel 11:35 says, that does not mean we are under God's wrath. God's wrath doesn't necessarily cover every square inch of the ground during the tribulation. There will be "saints" on the earth during that time and even if you accept for the moment that the Church is gone it is clear that at least these "saints" are differentiated from those who are under God's wrath. If these "saints" can be spared wrath during the time of wrath, why couldn't the whole church? This verse is proof of nothing.

Another verse is Matthew 16:18. "And I say also unto thee, That thou art Peter, and upon this rock I will build my church; and the gates of hell *shall not prevail against it.*" This verse is contrasted with Daniel 7:21 where it says the "horn" made war with the saints and *prevailed* against them, and Revelation 13:7 where it says the beast of the bottomless pit shall make war with them and *overcome* them. The argument is, if Jesus said the gates of hell shall not prevail against the Church, then how could the man antichrist be able to prevail against it? Clearly, this is not the Church that he is prevailing against and, therefore, the Church must have been raptured out.

First, once again there is no mention whatsoever in this verse of any kind of rapture. This is just a reaching attempt to find something to justify a pre-conceived notion. The logical failure of the argument lies in their inability or unwillingness to distinguish between being overcome physically and overcome spiritually. The man antichrist will most definitely persecute the Church and prophecy makes it clear many will be killed. They will be "overcome." But on a spiritual level, the writings also make it abundantly clear that the Church will overcome the man antichrist and the designs of Satan. This is stated in Revelation 12:11, "And they *overcame him* by the blood of the Lamb, and by the word of their testimony; and they loved not their lives unto the death." To fail to see this distinction between prevailing physically and prevailing spiritually is to be intellectually dishonest.

Other texts used to justify the idea of the rapture before the "tribulation" include the stories of Noah and the ark and Lot and Sodom and Gomorrah. The argument is that in both cases the "righteous" were taken out before a great judgment of destruction was carried out. Therefore, the Church will be raptured out before the great judgment of the tribulation. These stories are true but that does not make them prophetic pictures of a "pre-tribulation" rapture. The parallels between these stories and the projected idea of a pre-tribulation rapture are obvious. But they are by no means proof or even an indication of anything of the sort. The Church is not going to be under judgment during the seven year period. Rather, they will be under persecution. Persecution is not something that the Lord commonly takes his people out of. If I understand the words of Jesus correctly, he said many times in the gospels that the saints would suffer persecution. Persecution is not judgment. Rather, the saints will be tried and purged and made white. (Daniel 11:35) On the other hand, the rapture *does* occur just prior to the final judgment of Christ and the battle of Armageddon. The saints *will* be taken out right at the end, just before Christ sets foot on the earth and destroys all the wicked. So in a sense, these type and shadow stories of Noah and Sodom really are reflective of God's "last minute" deliverance.

But putting all of that aside, the fact that none of the chronological narratives of end times events mention anything that could be even remotely interpreted as a gathering of the saints at any other time than the end of the seven years, just before the return of Christ, makes the claim that these stories indicate such an event before the seven years without credibility.

2 Thessalonians 2:6-10

This reference is really a reach. It says, "And now ye know what withholdeth that he might be revealed in his time. For the mystery of iniquity doth already work: only he who now letteth will let, until he be taken out of the way, and then shall that Wicked be revealed…even him who's coming is after the working of Satan …"

Ok, this verse is clearly speaking of the man antichrist, the wicked whom the Lord shall consume with the spirit of his mouth. But who is it talking about that must be taken out of the way? First, let me help you with the old English use of "let" and "letteth." In reality, the Greek word translated here as "let" or "letteth" is the same Greek word that was translated "witholdeth" in the sentence just preceding it. In other words, the one who has the authority to "let" or "allow" is also the same one that has authority to "not allow" or to "withhold." So basically, it's just saying he that has authority to withhold will continue to withhold until he is taken out of the way. Then the man antichrist will be revealed.

The Dispensationalist says that the "he" that "withholds" is the Holy Spirit that only resides on the earth by indwelling the saints of the Church. When the Church is raptured out the Holy Spirit will go with it. Only then can the man antichrist be revealed.

There are some huge assumptions in this idea. It is true that the Holy Spirit indwells the saints of the Church. But after that the "logic" falls apart. Where does the idea come from that the Holy Ghost (HG) only inhabits the earth because he inhabits the Church or would somehow be excluded from the earth just because the Church was taken out? There are many examples of people being filled with the Holy Ghost before the Church of Jesus Christ began and God is everywhere at all times. The HG is not going to disappear from the earth just because the Church does.

But ignoring that for a moment, if you didn't already have the premise of a change in dispensation, why would anyone assume that this person or thing that is preventing the appearance of the man antichrist is the Holy Spirit? There is nothing in this verse that remotely suggests such a thing. Besides, the spirit of antichrist is rapidly dominating the peoples of the whole world and it doesn't appear the current presence of the Church and the Holy Spirit is doing a lot to prevent it. This idea is a huge assumption or speculation that is now taught as indisputable truth because it fits their invented theology. But it makes no sense in light of all of the other positive proof texts of when the rapture takes place.

I don't know who this text is referring to. Perhaps it is an angelic force. There are other references in Revelation to angels that are holding back actions until the appointed time. Look at Revelation 7:1-3. Granted, this is a speculation on my part. But it is more reasonable than saying it is the Holy Ghost that must be taken out along with the Church. Paul spoke openly about the rapture in I Thessalonians 4:16-17 and 1 Corinthians 15:51-52. Why would he suddenly get cryptic and mysterious here?

And besides all of this, even if this idea was valid, this would place the rapture in the middle of the seven year period, not at the beginning, because the man antichrist does not come on the scene until the middle. The error of the Dispensationalist comes from his misinterpretation of Daniel 9:27. As we discussed earlier, the "he" in the original language text refers to "the people" of antichrist and the idea of "covenant" refers to Israel and not some new peace treaty. The Dispensationalist, however, believes the "he" refers to the man antichrist that supposedly authors this new peace treaty with Israel. This places him on the scene from the beginning. But all of the other prophecies concerning the man antichrist place him as coming on the scene in the middle, when he uproots the three horns (kings) and sets up the abomination of desolation. So the whole idea that 2 Thessalonians 2:6-10 suggests a rapture of the Church at the beginning of the seven year period is simply not substantiated by any other prophecy or by any reasonable assumptions concerning what or who Paul was referring to. At the very least, if you did not already have the pre-conceived notion that there had to be a rapture at the beginning of the seven year period, you most certainly would not gather that idea from this text.

Given the many proof texts shown above for a post tribulation rapture and showing the fallacies of the dispensational arguments, I once again say that I am amazed that there is any controversy on this subject. The rapture occurs at the end of the seven year period, just following the sign of the Son of Man in the sky as he returns in the clouds with the voice of the archangel and the trump of God, and just prior to his setting foot on the earth to cleanse the earth of all evil. There are no verses in the writings that refer to or even suggest a rapture of the Church of any kind will occur at any other time. To teach that there are is to prophesy out of the imagination of one's own heart and not the writings of prophecy.

Made in the USA
Coppell, TX
29 October 2019

10650854R00113